Surviving Panic Disorder

What You Need to Know

By

Stuart Shipko, M.D.

ISBN: 1-4107-8735-4 (e-book)
ISBN: 1-4107-8734-6 (Paperback)

Library of Congress Control Number: 2003096871

This book is printed on acid free paper.

Printed in the United States of America
Bloomington, IN

1stBooks — rev. 10/07/03

Introduction

In 1836 after finishing a 5-year scientific excursion to South America and the Pacific, Charles Darwin, returned to England to find himself almost housebound. Doctors could not find a diagnosis for Darwin's problems that included an overwhelming sensation of fear, palpitations, weakness and muscle tremor that overcame him whenever he left home. After making a rare speech at a scientific meeting he was reported to have had 24 hours of vomiting. Remarking on his response to stress, The Life and Letters of Charles Darwin, cites Darwin having written, "...of late anything which flurries me completely knocks me up afterwards, and brings on violent palpitation of the heart."

Darwin probably had panic disorder. Today, he would not have had to suffer as he did, however it is likely that he would need to be an informed consumer of healthcare to get proper treatment.

I am a board certified psychiatrist who specializes in panic disorder. Over the last twenty years I have personally examined and treated well over 2,000 patients with panic disorder. In 1996 I put up the Panic Disorders Institute (PDI) web site. Besides presenting basic information on panic disorder, the web site has a bulletin board where people can post questions. The people who post these questions are usually under the care of physicians, but in addition to their physician's advice they are seeking to become as educated as possible about panic disorder. Self-education is an essential part of any treatment for panic disorder. This is particularly true for the confusing psychosomatic aspects of panic disorder.

In addition to my clinical experience the years of reading and answering the questions on the bulletin board has helped me to understand what information is needed most by people with panic disorder. In this book I will share my knowledge and experience with patients and their physicians. Panic disorder is an increasingly popular diagnosis. The actual incidence of panic disorder is probably rising but it is also progressively more popular with medical and mental health practitioners and often given out casually to people who do not have it.

"Panic attack" is a label used to describe almost any episodic medical condition that is frightening and otherwise difficult to explain. It is part of our common vocabulary and people commonly describe themselves as having a panic attack whenever they have intense anxiety. People may go to their doctors and tell them that they have had a panic attack, and the doctor may initiate treatment for panic disorder taking them at face value. Even so, a panic attack is not in itself always abnormal. Sometimes a panic attack is just an uncomfortable part of being human and sometimes it is part of a larger condition that requires medical attention.

Because the diagnostic features of panic disorder are completely descriptive one is technically correct to call a wide variety of physical sensations and emotional fears panic disorder. The disorder exists on a spectrum, with patients experiencing scary thoughts on one end and seizure-like neurological events on the other. For this reason, people who are told that they have panic disorder or think that they might have panic disorder find it bewildering when they try to get more information.

Beyond a summary of the literature on panic disorder, I share my medical approach to identifying and dealing with the key issues that face the person who may have panic disorder. My opinions are primarily based on my own clinical experience in dealing with panic

disorder. Panic disorder can be seen from a variety of viewpoints and

other clinicians may have valid opinions that differ from my own. All

clinical impressions are inherently subjective, embedded as they are

in the art of clinical medicine. Subjectivity aside, this is the

information most requested by my patients, and that is of most value

to the readers.

Posted September 2001to the PDI bulletin board by Rhonda:
> *Recently I found your website and I can't thank you enough. I have had horrible heartburn and panic attacks for years. I get frequent sinus infections, migraine headaches and have mitral valve prolapse. You were the first doctor to tie it all together for me. Thanks again.*

Few medical conditions are associated with such a wide range

of symptoms and associated medical problems. This is frustrating for

patients because physicians look at each symptom or condition as a

separate problem.

After examining in detail a large number of patients with

panic disorder, I formed a significantly different view of the condition

than any text or article has ever presented. It is not only an episodic

disease of attacks and phobias. It also includes a variety of ongoing neurological and medical problems, personal, family and emotional difficulties, gastroesophageal reflux and insomnia. Beyond symptoms people with panic disorder seem more sensitive to stress, emotions, relationships and foods.

Patients with panic disorder often have so many problems that they don't get the chance to discuss them all with their doctors. When patients tell doctors about too many symptoms at one time, the doctor becomes overwhelmed and tries to cut the interview short. At first, I too experienced the frustration of trying to listen to patients who had too many problems. It was maddening from the standpoint of proper medical practice where we systematically evaluate each complaint. As the patients told me about chest pain I considered a cardiology consultation and a series of tests to be ordered. As they told me about headaches and dizziness I considered a neurology or ENT consultation and another series of tests to be ordered. As they told me about insomnia I considered the need for a referral to a sleep disorder laboratory. It was impossible to order all the tests and make all of the referrals that the patient's complaints suggested.

As I saw more patients with panic disorder, I became better able to sift through symptoms and order appropriate evaluations, but this required that I spend hours on each new patient. The information gained in that manner was multiplied many-fold by the bulletin board on my website. Patients would exchange support and information on a variety of topics. Many of the same topics tended to recur every few months and I developed an understanding of just what information patients needed most. I answered questions and used the board to enhance my knowledge of this condition by posting my own questions and starting discussions. In this way I learned of many aspects of panic disorder that patients and doctors don't usually discuss, which made me rethink the nature of the condition.

Despite my experience I still find that panic disorder is not easy to understand. It not only straddles the line between mind and body, within the body it straddles several different medical specialties. A person might only have physical symptoms with no real sense of anxiety or enormous anxiety with only minor somatic symptoms. It is not a single disease. It is a group of conditions that have in common episodes of seemingly inexplicable physical and emotional symptoms and the aggravation of these symptoms through anticipation.

Acknowlegements

First I want to thank my wife, Mary Jane Horton for her love, encouragement and her editing skills. I am grateful to DL Hurley who organized the postings of the citizen scientists who have contributed to the Panic Disorders Institute website. I thank Steve Ward for helping to promote my research. Thanks to Jill Gannon for her early help and Muriel Nellis for her encouragement and constructive criticism. Thanks to John Mandel for listening to me while we jog. Thanks to my patients who have been so supportive. Thank you Melvin and Karla Fishman. I want to thank my children, Zachary and Chloe. Finally I want to thank my parents, Albert and Dorothy Shipko who provided me with life and education.

Contents

Chapter I: My Journey

The training of the medical school gives man his direction, points him the way, and furnishes him with a chart, fairly incomplete, for the voyage, but nothing more.

Sir William Osler: Aphorisms from His Bedside Teachings and Writings

My interest in panic disorder began in the early 70's while I was in medical school at the University of Michigan. I noticed that a large percentage of patients had anxiety-provoking symptoms and problems for which there was no explanation. Patients were told, "it is all in your head" or "it's just stress" or "don't worry about it." The idea of emotional stress causing physical illness fascinated me. It was clear to me that emotional discomfort should cause emotional distress, but it was not at all clear to me how mental distress caused physical illnesses.

This prompted me to study stress physiology. I received a small National Institute of Science grant to do research on the effects of adrenaline, the fight or flight hormone, on the vascular system. My research in the field of stress physiology shed some light on the mind-body connection but still did not explain what I saw in the medical clinics. Furthermore, I observed that the physicians were condescending and unkind to people who had stress or anxiety related problems, as if they were wasting the doctor's time.

The mind-body connection fascinated me and I wanted a residency that would allow me to study it further. Unfortunately no such residency existed. Family medicine and Internal medicine residencies were rigid and gave little or no education in the area of psychosomatic medicine. It was only in the field of psychiatry that I was able to find the flexibility I needed to work in a multidisciplinary area like stress disease. Boston University allowed me to design a combined clinical/research residency that would allow me to pursue research in the field of psychosomatic medicine.

I went to Boston and started my general internship at the Framingham Union Hospital, a community hospital affiliated with Boston University. They told me to get accustomed to the internship and living in Boston and then we would discuss my proposed research. After a month or two I called the residency directors to set an appointment to discuss my research. They told me flatly, "You don't need an appointment, since you will not do any research for three years anyway. Then you will have a half day a week for your project."

Disenchanted, I decided that I wanted nothing to do with the silliness of psychiatry. Instead I went into the practical world of emergency medicine. Working in the emergency room I was struck, again, with the phenomenon of people who felt that they were having strokes, heart attacks and a myriad of conditions for which no physical cause could be found. Patients who had these sorts of problems were called somatizers, referring to the idea that they were taking their emotional problems and expressing them in their bodies. These patients were viewed as a waste of the doctor's time, and my fellow physicians were all to happy to direct suspected somatizers to me. As the junior member of my group I had more night and graveyard shifts than my partners and the somatizers were also more common in the night and early morning. Most of these were people having panic attacks, however this was before the name panic attack had been invented.

Often these "worried well" were the most difficult and time-consuming patients. I started studying them. Besides doing the usual diagnostic evaluations, I also studied therapeutic interventions to better treat these patients. After a while I developed a protocol using gestalt techniques that seemed very promising. I would mirror their symptom with questions that elicited a catharsis, and symptoms would resolve. For example, I would ask the man with chest pressure if there was something he wanted to get off his chest; the woman who couldn't swallow if she had something in her life that was tough to swallow, the person with tremor if they had an experience that shook him up. Often, in their eagerness to discuss their emotions, the patients forgot to even ask if their medical tests were normal. In quite a few cases, they left the emergency department with their symptoms completely resolved.

I felt as if I had made a discovery of enormous value and I wanted to study this in greater depth. Having written up a number of these cases I composed a research protocol to refine and study my treatment for emergency somatizers. The University of California at Irvine department of psychiatry accepted me into their residency program and we arranged for an individualized program of combined research and clinical training.

My enthusiasm for this research was enormous because I thought that my treatment for emergency somatizers was both simple and revolutionary. Meeting with the emergency room director, I set up a structured protocol. After their doctors had determined that the patient had no medical illness, I would be called in and use this technique of mirroring the symptom in language. I carried a beeper just for the emergency department and would frequently be called out of lectures and meetings to go to the emergency room for my project. Frankly, almost all of my time was going into various aspects of this research project and I did only the minimum required of me to comply with other residency requirements. My study of psychiatry revolved primarily around the mind body connection.

To my complete surprise, the mirroring technique was a total disappointment. After a few months I stopped my research completely. What had seemed so helpful and promising when I was an emergency doctor fell completely flat when I was a psychiatric consultant. It was a dismal failure: it didn't work for anyone, and the patients, despite my courtesy and interest, often resented me.

I needed to find out why the exact same maneuver that seemed so promising when executed as an emergency doctor seemed so utterly useless when performed as a psychiatrist. The only real difference was me: now I was a psychiatrist and before I was an ER doctor.

I realized that as a psychiatrist the patients saw me as a person who was delving directly into their emotions, but as an emergency doctor I was making a sneak attack into their emotions.

Looking into the literature on emotions, I read about the concept of alexithymia. Alexithymia is thought to be a disconnection between the physical and mental aspects of emotion. Alexithymics complain endlessly of physical problems for which no physical cause can be found. The physical symptoms actually get worse when alexithymics are treated by psychotherapy. This seemed to explain what had occurred. As a psychiatrist my intervention was viewed by the patient as psychotherapy.

I went back to the patients who I saw in my research project and I administered a scale that would measure alexithymia. These patients almost all rated as profoundly alexithymic on psychometric testing as well as on a repeated clinical interview looking for alexithymic characteristics. It was of interest that most of the patients had had their symptom for over five years. The patient who rated the most alexithymic had been going to emergency rooms for 20 years for a "funny" sensation in his head. In his last visit he told the doctor that he had a stomach pain because he was embarrassed to say that he was having that feeling in his head that had been evaluated so many times before. He figured that if he had *anything* life threatening that the doctors would find it no matter what he complained about.

As I studied what I then called "alexithymic emergency somatizers" I was struck by the fact that while they did complain of physical sensations of pain or discomfort for which medicine had no explanation, they were also less sensitive to induced pain.

Clinically, the blunted sensation of induced pain seemed to be quite pronounced. Setting out to study this I set up an experiment in which I looked at pain tolerance in alexithymic and non-alexithymic

7

groups. Thin plastic patches with imbedded wires that conducted heat were placed over the fingertips of people who had taken psychometric tests to assess for alexithymia. The electric current that caused the heat could be quantified on a 1 to 10 scale. The more alexithymic half of the people studied were less sensitive to thermal pain, but this was just short of statistical significance.

Still, I felt that this was enough to provide objective support for the subjective reports of the somatizing patients that they were less affected by painful stimuli.

Looking again at the literature, I thought I'd found an explanation based on inescapable stress, which is mediated by the endorphins, the body's natural opiates. When rats were repeatedly administered electric shock they became less sensitive to these shocks due to endorphin release. This model certainly seemed to fit the patients that I had seen. Many of them had been traumatized and became numb. Combat veterans were highly alexithymic as a group. The emotional numbing of trauma was nothing new; Freud had written of this more than a century ago.

What I could not reconcile was the idea that the same people who were presumably opiated as a result of stress were also the people who showed up in the emergency room late at night sure that they were having a heart attack. How could they feel more pain and less pain at the same time?

For eight years I would go to sleep at night asking myself this question: how is it that stressed out, opiated people who were less sensitive to induced pain were also more sensitive to internal sensations of pain, particularly at night.

The answer arrived piecemeal. In 1983 and 1984 Linda Watkins et al published an article in *Science*, which described reversal of stress-induced analgesia by cholecystokinin (CCK), released after conditions of stress were over. When laboratory rats were repeatedly given electric shocks they released endorphins as expected. The rats were trained to learn cues that would tell them when the series of electric shocks were completed. If given these cues after the shocks ended the rats released CCK. CCK is a hormone and brain chemical that is known to cause panic attacks when injected into the blood stream.

This model of inescapable stress seems to fit the day-to-day life stresses that we all experience. While not so traumatic as electric shock, the ongoing stress of daily life needs to be endured until it is over. We cannot escape our commute, our jobs, driving the kids to soccer, our relationships. We tend to be busy all day long, and often do not have the chance to unstress until sleep.

Opiates are released while under stress and CCK is released after stress ends. This model suggests that alexithymic somatizers are numb from the endorphins when under stress, but after stress is over CCK release results in panic attacks.

Because CCK is also the primary stimulus for bile flow, it seemed logical that panic attacks would be associated with excessive bile flow. My own research confirmed this. Panic disorder patients tended to have excessive bile flow at night. Clinically the abnormal bile flow resulted in gastritis and gastroesophageal reflux with its extraesophageal manifestations of sinusitis, throat problems and breathing difficulties.

In the early 90's, having finished a body of research linking gastroesophageal reflux and panic disorder I presented this at major gastroenterology meetings. It was not an efficient way to reach the millions of people who were under psychiatric care for panic disorder and who also had reflux. I considered presenting this data at psychiatry meetings but realized that psychiatrists are not going to practice what seems like gastroenterology. In medicine, the physician is obligated to refer to other specialists when confronting a problem outside of their own specialty.

The Internet proved to be an efficient vehicle for getting this information to the people who needed it. I had underestimated the number of people who had panic disorder and reflux and were looking for the connection between the two. Thousands of people who had problems related to both reflux and panic disorder contacted me. They intuitively knew that their reflux and their panic disorder were one condition. As my understanding of panic disorder matured it became clear that this was just the beginning. Panic disorder was associated with an even larger constellation of medical conditions.

Opening this work to the Internet had far-reaching consequences. My practice was altered because people would seek me out specifically for the treatment of panic and reflux. In 1998 I left my hospital practice to concentrate almost exclusively on panic disorder. At this time the Internet was becoming a common fixture in people's lives and the discussion board on my website, Panic Disorders Institute (PDI), became much more popular. This logarithmically expanded the information sent to me concerning the needs and unaddressed problems of people with panic disorder. A group of highly educated patients who I affectionately refer to as "citizen scientists" had the skill and the generosity to share valuable personal and scientific insights on the PDI bulletin board. As I studied and responded to those who wrote to the bulletin board, I began to see two basic themes. First, we were consistently several steps ahead of the medical mainstream which, in its haste to treat this "disorder," had failed to take the vital first step of completely defining it. Second, the new antidepressants, touted as the cure for panic disorder, had an unacceptably high set of side effects. I had the kind of long term, personal access to the eye of the panic hurricane that a clinical researcher could only dream of. I was in daily cyber-contact with a multitude of panic sufferers—far more than I could possibly see as patients. Their range of experience—the commonalities and the differences—reinforced my belief that there was no "cure" for

panic disorder and that it may not be a disease at all so much as a

manifestation of an overtaxed nervous system.

Chapter II: I'm Falling Apart

Case Study: Is this panic disorder?
Maureen, a 43 year old nurse showed up at my office emotionally distraught. As soon as she sat down, she started to cry. "I'm falling apart and my doctor tells me not to worry. Nobody seems to understand what I am going through and I feel like I am going to jump out of my skin."

Initially, she went to her family doctor because of chest pain. She had other symptoms as well; shortness of breath, palpitations, perspiration and a feeling that she was going to die or collapse at any second. To some people these symptoms would constitute panic attacks, but to Maureen they were parts of an even larger picture.

"I wake up the same time each night, about 3AM with severe heartburn. It doesn't matter what I've had for dinner and I don't eat before sleep. I can't get back to sleep. I worry about not sleeping and being tired in the morning. It seems like the more tired I am from the day, the more heartburn I have and the worse I sleep. Without sleep I feel tired all the time and it seems as if my joints hurt also."

Part of Maureen's confusion is that some of her problems were not new. She told me that she had had a period of several months when she had panic attacks in her 20's. These attacks started about a week after the death of a great aunt. Maureen had not seen her for years. Her aunt was in her 90's had been ill in and was living

in a nursing home. Even so, this event seemed to trigger a stress

reaction in Maureen. When she was in her 20's all she noticed was

the panic attacks and the experience seemed quite different than it was

now.

"It surprised me how her death affected me because it was a blessing when she passed on," she said.

She also mentioned that as long as she could remember, she

became abnormally irritable during the premenstrual part of her cycle

and that at times she had felt depressed and had even thought about

suicide.

Maureen paused for a moment and asked me if I would think

she was crazy if she told me about another distressing problem she

had had over the years. She was not sure whether or not this was

relevant. She was tentative because in the past doctors had told her

that this problem was imaginary.

I know this sounds silly, but it sometimes when I wake up, whether it is in the middle of the night or the morning, often it seems as if I am awake, but I can't move my body for a few minutes. It feels like I am paralyzed.

Then I asked if she had any other "silly" symptoms. Tearfully

she replied,

"Lately I have a numb feeling on the left half of my body. It comes and goes, but the whole left side feels different for days at a time. I've had this on and off for about 10 years. It's not so numb that I can't feel anything, but things feel different on the left side. This is a lot worse if I go to get my hair done, and my husband has to cut my hair. I went to a neurologist and he told me this was "impossible" and not to worry about it. But I do worry about it; I worry that I might have multiple sclerosis or something. This doesn't make sense. What is wrong with me?"

This is a typical presentation for panic disorder although it is

not the only way it presents. In this case Maureen has a multiplicity

of problems including nocturnal panic attacks, heartburn, and sleep

paralysis. It is common for women to feel worse when going to get

her hair done. She is tired. To be sure she is also having panic

attacks, but in the context of all of the other symptoms that she has,

the panic attacks are only a small part of the problem. It feels to

Maureen that she is falling apart, that almost everything in her body,

and possibly her mind, isn't working. As a nurse she realizes that she

needs to see a different medical specialist for each problem, but this is

simply not practical when you need five or more medical

specialists—getting all of the medical examinations would become a career. At the same time Maureen has a sense that the symptoms that she has must be all part of a collective problem, but what could it be?

Panic disorder frequently is associated with a variety of medical and emotional problems beyond the symptoms of panic attacks themselves. A person such as Maureen may well need several different medical specialty examinations to insure that she does not have a variety of separate illnesses. It is confusing and anxiety provoking when it seems that many different unrelated medical problems are occurring simultaneously. The patient feels as if they are falling apart and wonders what is going to happen next. Knowing that the different symptoms are all pieces of the same puzzle is reassuring. Knowing what sorts of symptoms to expect is essential.

What is called panic disorder goes far beyond mere anxiety. Patients have a large variety of symptoms that are physical. Any part of the body that is regulated by electrical nervous activity is prone to malfunction. For this reason it is important to have a single physician who coordinates necessary specialty evaluations and then implements the specialist recommendations.

Chapter III: You are Not Alone

People who have panic disorder often have a profound sense that nobody—not friends, family or physicians understand how they are feeling. This is based, at least partially, in reality since most people do not understand how people with panic disorder feel.

Case study, Paula

Paula, a 45 year old court reporter, was having a panic attack at work. Paula began to feel as if she were going to pass out. Perspiring and tremulous she was unable to continue typing. She thought that somebody around her must see that she was in such great distress. "I felt as if my head was going to explode," she told the bailiff. She was expecting him to call an ambulance. He replied, "I get this all the time, just take some aspirin." I told him that I have never had this before and I think I need an ambulance. He just smiled and handed me some aspirin."

Often family and friends see panic attacks as an overreaction to the usual fears we all face. They have no frame of reference with which to relate to the panic experience except their own experience with fear. They may view panic disorder as a moral weakness or a manipulative behavior. Well meaning family and friends may encourage you to be "less high strung" or to "get a grip on yourself." The classic phrase that induces shame, rage and failure is, "I had that too, you know, and I got over it." This is hardly a comfort to someone who is in the grip of a body and mind spinning out of control. The person feels weak and ashamed and wonders why they are not able to get over it as well.

Furthermore, physicians have been given only a vague description of this condition and have equally vague and sometimes inappropriate ideas on how to diagnose or treat it. A significant number of doctors do not even believe that panic disorder is a separate entity from other types of anxiety. They consider a panic attack to be an experience of high anxiety. Physical problems that are difficult to diagnose are being called panic attacks. Increasingly, I see patients who have physical symptoms that are difficult to diagnose misdiagnosed as panic disorder.

Panic disorder occurs in an estimated 1 out of 75 people worldwide. Some people have it starting in early childhood, while in others panic attacks start in the late teens and early 20's. Although the condition usually shows itself by early adulthood, it may not be apparent until middle age and rarely has an onset over 60. Commonly it is first experienced as a physical disturbance and it is often confusing to doctor and patient alike. The experience of a panic attack is generally more physical than emotional and it is common to fear that these spells represent undiagnosed medical conditions such as a seizure or heart disease. A considerable number of emergency room visits and a considerable number of all physician visits are panic related. Patients may be seeing a variety of doctors for different physical problems who have not put these problems together into the single diagnosis of panic disorder. It is not uncommon for patients with panic disorder to go to as many as 10 different medical specialists before being correctly diagnosed.

As common as this problem may be, people who have panic disorder have a strong sense of being different. They look around at the people in their lives and have the sense that nobody has problems like they do and they feel as if they are inadequate and unable to cope with what is clearly average.

Coping and adjusting is more difficult for the person with panic disorder, however, the experience of panic disorder is best described as an exaggeration of the experience of stress. The experience of panic disorder is something that all people feel,

21

although it is more prominent in someone with panic disorder. Trust

me, you are definitely not alone.

Chapter IV: The Panic Attack Defined

Part of the problem with diagnosis is that while panic disorders share a variety of symptoms in common, they are all slightly different from each other. Every snowflake is unique, but they are nonetheless still easily identifiable as snowflakes. Similarly no two cases of panic disorder are going to be exactly the same, however they are still identifiable as panic disorder.

The DSM—IV, the Diagnostic and Statistical Manual for the American Psychiatric Association, fourth edition, gives a very basic definition of panic disorder. It is important to realize that the disorders described in this manual are not descriptions of actual diseases. These sorts of classifications reflect a consensus of evolving knowledge of psychiatric illnesses. It was created in order to standardize the definitions of various syndromes in order to enable clinicians to effectively communicate with each other about specific illnesses. It is not intended to be a complete description of any disorder nor does it imply any physiologic cause for the disorders. The classification of panic disorder describes a diverse group of problems from a variety of causes that share certain features. The DSM—IV criterion for this disorder are fairly simple. Understanding the larger picture of panic disorder is not quite so simple, but first lets look at these criterion.

Criterion are met when a person has recurrent *unexpected* panic attacks (or at least one) and at least one month of worry about having additional panic attacks or worry about the significance of the attacks or avoidance behaviors that result from the attacks.

A panic attack is defined as a discrete period of intense fear or discomfort, peaking within about 10 minutes that is associated with 4 of 13 identified symptoms. The 13 symptoms are:

• sense of rapid or forceful heart beat

• perspiration

• tremor

• shortness of breath or a sensation of smothering

• feeling of choking

• chest pain or discomfort

• nausea or abdominal distress

• feeling dizzy, unsteady, lightheaded or faint

• feeling that the immediate environment is not real or that one is detached from oneself

• fear of losing control or going crazy

• fear of dying

• tingling of the extremities

• chills or hot flashes

It is doubtful that the doctor will be taking the history with this checklist in mind. Most doctors would not be able to recite by memory the criterion for a panic attack. Usually doctors think of a panic attack as any sudden and overwhelming sense of fear usually associated with chest pain, shortness of breath and lightheadedness. Hearing that a patient has gone to an emergency room and has been told that they have no problem leads most physicians to suspect that the visit was for a panic attack. In the emergency room or in the office a person has any abrupt, anxiety provoking physical symptoms that are unexplainable by tests or X-rays then doctors are likely to call this a panic attack.

Chapter V: Unexpected v. Situational Attacks

By definition a panic attack occurs "out of the blue." This is a value judgment as it may be difficult to tell whether or not an attack is cued by a seeming danger or if it happens spontaneously. A person usually experiences a panic attack as a stress response and expects this sort of experience *during* stressful situations. When a person is relaxing and they have a panic attack it is unexpected. This is counterintuitive because a person expects to react to stress when it is happening, not afterward.

There is, however, a pattern to the unexpected panic attacks. They tend to occur following a period of stress or activity. Our nervous system accelerates and prepares for activity well, but is unstable when moving from stress to relaxation. States of nervous system instability seem to be most closely associated with symptoms of anxiety.

So when we speak of an unexpected or spontaneous attack, we are speaking from the frame of reference of the patient.

Panic attacks occur in many different emotional states. For diagnostic purposes, one needs to consider the relationship between the onset of the attack and the presence or absence of situational triggers. The panic attacks of panic disorder are *not supposed to be associated with a situational trigger.* They supposedly occur spontaneously, unexpectedly or "out of the blue." Panic attacks from other forms of anxiety are supposed to occur in response to a thought, a situation or anticipation of a situation.

The distinction between unexpected panic attacks and situational panic attacks is not entirely clear. Some people experience what seems like an unexpected attack but can really be responding to their own repressed unconscious thoughts. For example, a person might have deeply repressed anger towards a parent and after a phone call with this parent develop a panic attack which seems out of the blue. In reality this panic attack would probably be an emotional reaction to the repressed rage towards the parent. Repressed conflict or rage of any sort can seem like a spontaneous panic attack. Also, people with a previous traumatic experience can have an anxiety reaction to something that unconsciously reminds them of the traumatic event and this will seem spontaneous as well.

Complicating this distinction even more, after a person has any sort of panic attack they commonly develop situational panic attacks to the cues that were present during the unexpected attack. For example, if an attack occurs while sitting in a movie, the person may later develop attacks cued by movie theaters or the thought of movie theatres. Most people with panic disorder will be having a mixture of the two types of panic attacks.

The diagnostic feature of panic disorder that clarifies the expected versus unexpected issue for me is the nocturnal attack. Panic attacks commonly wake people up out of sleep and these nocturnal panic attacks are present in most people with panic disorder. Surprisingly not all physicians are aware that panic attacks even occur during sleep. Nocturnal panic attacks are often associated with symptoms of reflux such as heartburn. People waking up with racing heart and shortness of breath may feel as if they are waking up from a nightmare, although the symptoms will persist significantly longer than what is usually associated with awakening from a nightmare.

This seems to be one of the clearest types of unexpected panic attacks, unprovoked by external cues.

The panic attacks of panic disorder are defined in the DSM-IV as "unexpected." But for practical purposes it remains very difficult to precisely establish what is internally or externally cued and what is completely unexpected.

The difference between what is expected and what is unexpected is highly subjective. For practical purposes this means that the panic attacks of panic disorder usually happen when relaxing or shortly after going to sleep. Attacks are unexpected by the patient because they occur when they are relaxing, not while under stress. In a given patient panic attacks tend to occur at roughly the same time of day. Most of the spontaneous panic attacks seem to happen in the late afternoon, evening and shortly after going to sleep. Activity and rest usually follow a 24 hour waking and sleeping rhythm and this is the case with panic attacks as well. In some circumstances a panic attack can occur in a different rhythm, after a person has been very busy for a period of weeks or more. For example, the sister of one of my patients died. The patient needed to fly across the country, make arrangements for a funeral, care for her sister's children and deal with the estate while making arrangements for the children's future care. This was exhausting. While dealing with all of this the patient was stressed but not having panic attacks. It was when she returned home, after this flurry of activity that a cluster of panic attacks developed.

Chapter VI: Features of Panic Attacks

Although the criteria for a panic attack describes an abrupt onset with symptoms peaking within 10 minutes, the time sequencing on these attacks can be highly variable. A panic attack has been described to me as if a switch to the stress reaction turned on. Others describe the onset as a surge of adrenalin. The onset of a panic attack is abrupt, not gradual. Most attacks do peak in 5 to 15 minutes, however some attacks can persist hours or even days.

Patients sometimes describe waves of panic attacks in which symptoms wax and wane over hours or days or sometimes weeks. Symptoms may ease, but never completely go away during a wave attack. When panic attacks come in waves over several days the person is usually unable to sleep, stops going to work and feels intensely uncomfortable.

Frequency of panic attacks is highly variable. Some people may have mild attacks once or twice a month; others may have severe attacks every day. Infrequent panic attacks are tolerated by many people and are not uncommon. Most people can tolerate an isolated panic attack from time to time. The most common reason for people to seek treatment is when panic attacks occur in clusters. When the condition is flaring, attacks will tend to occur several times a week or even more frequently. Attacks are most often discrete, not in waves, but can occur as often as several times in a 24-hour period. Even two or three attacks a week is enough to be incapacitating. When attacks are in clusters or waves people usually seek prompt attention. In these situations the symptoms are extremely uncomfortable and well out of the range of any ordinary physical or mental discomfort.

Further Description of Some Panic Attack Symptoms

Panic attacks have been referred to as the great pretender because symptoms are so varied and complex. The symptoms described below are the major ones that patients encounter but by no means all of the symptoms that may be a part of a panic attack.

Shortness of Breath - Hyperventilation

This is one of the most common symptoms and is highly variable. In some people it is a sense that they cannot get a full breath. They feel unsatisfied with the sensation of a deep breath—it simply doesn't feel deep enough. Others describe that their throat feels as if it has closed down and they are trying to breathe through a small straw with great effort.

In some cases breathing feels out of control with rapid and deep respirations happening as if the breathing control mechanism is stuck on fast speed. When this occurs, people will feel symptoms of hyperventilation such as tingling of the arms, legs and around the face and mouth. When hyperventilation is pronounced, then a condition called carpal pedal spasm can occur. This is when hyperventilation leads to a shift in blood chemistry causing muscle activity resulting in the wrists bending and the hands clenching like claws. Similarly the feet may go into spasm. This is frightening but not dangerous. It goes away after hyperventilation stops.

Besides feeling as if getting enough air is impossible, some people feel it is impossible to forget about breathing. When they try to breathe automatically they can't. They find that breathing is only possible as an intentional act. When this happens people do not stop breathing because they "forget" to breath. Rather they have an inability to stop thinking about breathing.

Some people may hyperventilate without a sense of disturbed respiration. They do not feel short of breath and feel as if they are breathing normally. Still, they are breathing faster than they need to and they develop the physical symptoms of hyperventilation, particularly tingling of the extremities and face. In more severe states of hyperventilation the hands and feet can go into spasm.

Tremor

Tremor may not always be visible. Sometimes people feel as if they are having a tremor but it is not visible to others. Usually tremor is minimal but occasionally it can be quite pronounced and visible. Tremor does not generally persist in between panic attacks.

Fear of Dying

While the *DSM IV* mentions fear of dying, patients more often tell me that they felt as if they were about to die not that they had a fear of dying. The distinction here is that a patient may not be having anxiety about death or fear of death so much as having a sensation that causes them to feel as if they are about to die. This has long been a curiosity to me because unless someone has had a near death experience, they would not know what it feels like to be about to die. Nevertheless I hear this from patients frequently.

Nausea or Abdominal Distress

The *DSM IV* criterion of nausea or abdominal distress is vague. Abdominal distress is too vague. It describes any gastrointestinal symptom. Nausea is a common feature of anxiety. Nausea can also be one of the symptoms associated with hyperventilation. In some people nausea can be quite severe. Patients with severe nausea may experience a secondary fear of vomiting. It is uncommon, but occasionally patients will actually throw up during a panic attack. Heartburn is probably the most common GI symptom that people describe. This is experienced as a burning sensation in the upper abdomen. Heartburn and reflux are present in almost everyone who has panic disorder, and not exclusively during a panic attack. Bloating and belching during attacks are also common symptoms.

Depersonalization and Derealization

Derealization is the sense that the environment is not real and depersonalization is the feeling that one is not attached to one's body. These are common feelings in people with anxiety and are also found in people who do not have anxiety. In depersonalization the person feels like they are not able to control speech and movement even as they observe themselves speaking and moving. They wonder how any movement at all is possible and may have a sense that they are looking at themselves from across the room. In derealization a person has the feeling that everything around them is not real, that it is either staged or dreamlike. The person retains contact with reality, but has the distinct sensation of unreality.

Feeling Faint and Dizzy

This bears special mention because some people actually do faint during panic attacks. Many doctors don't know about this and they may fail to make the proper diagnosis. Fear of fainting is much more common than actually fainting.

Dizziness is one of the most common symptoms during the attacks and often, to a lesser degree, between attacks. It usually feels like a sense of being off balance. At times the room may feel as if it is shaking as if an earthquake was happening. The feelings of faintness and dizziness often occur simultaneously. Vertigo is the sensation that the room is spinning. Vertigo is uncommon as a primary symptom of panic attacks although it can cause intense anxiety.

Anger and Crying Attacks

Anger attacks, more commonly found in men, are an atypical form of panic attack. They have an intense and abrupt onset and tend to last about 20 minutes. When people are intensely angry they do not notice racing heart or hyperventilation. Some panic attacks are characterized by anger only. Intense crying spells, more commonly found in women, are another atypical form of panic attack.

Reflux

Reflux is a major part of the experience of panic disorder. It often causes as much discomfort as panic attacks. Gastroesophageal reflux happens when gastric contents move backwards from the stomach into the esophagus. When it's symptomatic it's usually called gastroesophageal reflux disease (GERD). Most commonly experienced as heartburn it also causes a variety of other symptoms such as sinusitis, throat irritation or, if it is aspirated into the lungs, it causes chronic cough and asthma.

Reflux is a very common problem in people with panic disorder. It may occur during panic attacks, between attacks or late at night, hours after the last meal.

In some people stomach discomfort is felt all the time. When this happens the patients may gradually come to experience the abdominal discomfort as anxiety.

Fatigue and Muscle Pain

Panic disorder has a strong overlap with chronic fatigue syndrome and fibromyalgia. In panic disorder commonly there is pain and spasm along the 'trigger points" of fibromyalgia. Usually this follows the borders of the trapezius muscle as well as in other soft tissues of the back and neck although joint and muscle pain can be found in many areas. Often people with panic disorder meet criterion for fibromyalgia or chronic fatigue syndrome or both. Because all three conditions are diagnosed by a descriptive list of symptoms and they overlap, this can get confusing. It is not uncommon for a person with panic disorder to also receive a diagnosis of chronic fatigue or fibromyalgia. Whether or not these are the same condition or separate but overlapping conditions has not been established at this time.

Incontinence

Another very common feature of panic disorder is urinary or fecal incontinence. Urinary incontinence and fecal incontinence are fairly common problems in panic disorder.

Abnormal bile flow is the usual cause of fecal incontinence. Bile released in the absence of food is quite caustic and the gut wants to pass it through quickly. Bile can pass through the entire small and large intestine in less than 15 minutes. Because bile is caustic it will tend to feel like it is burning on defecation. Usually the fecal incontinence tends to be very small in quantity.

A sense of urinary urgency is fairly common and actual loss of urine is less common but still occurs. Usually the fear of incontinence is the greater problem. It would be great to tell a patient that fear of incontinence is totally unfounded. The truth is that it does occasionally occur.

Chapter VII: Agoraphobia

The *DSM IV* describes panic disorder with and without agoraphobia. Agoraphobia is derived from the Greek language and literally translated means "fear of the market place." Agoraphobia is defined as anxiety about being in places or situations from which escape might be difficult or where help might not be available in the event of panic-like symptoms. The DSM—IV cites examples of this, being outside of the home alone, standing in a line, being in a crowd or crossing a bridge. Situations of being confined or trapped are avoided or are tolerated with significant discomfort.

In my experience when a person has panic attacks, agoraphobia is always present to some degree. I have also seen symptoms similar to agoraphobia in every medical problem that is episodic and intensely uncomfortable. People with episodic problems are always concerned about possibly having another episode and whether or not they will have resources to deal with it. In the presence of uncontrolled episodic problems it is natural for a person to stay close to home. These behaviors are not always related to a

43

need to escape or to have help in the event of a panic attack. Often staying in a safe place is an almost unconscious attempt to prevent symptoms.

Commonly avoided spaces include enclosed spaces such as the shower or elevators. Getting a haircut or getting dental work done is often avoided. Driving the freeway is probably the single most avoided event. Avoidance behaviors may extend to eating certain foods or to taking any type of medication. Crowds, lines, supermarkets and unfamiliar social situations are usually a problem as well. Whenever a person with panic disorder is confronted with a novel situation, one that requires a change from the usual patterns of activity the tendency will be to avoid this change, even if it is a pleasant event, such as a vacation.

Avoidance behaviors can be directed towards a variety of objects and situations but is most commonly directed towards locations. The agoraphobic person will have locations that feel unsafe and locations that feel safe and this is usually not based on logical concerns. People can, at times, become housebound and can become limited to even a single room in their house, but global avoidance of all outside locations is less common than avoidance of specific locations. Distance from home affects some people who find that they are fine until they get to a certain limit, such as 1 mile, 10 miles, 20 miles, or even 100 miles from home. Once the point of comfort is exceeded it is as if the person has hit a wall.

Often people with agoraphobia feel more comfortable when they are with a companion. It would seem logical that a person who fears sudden physical collapse would want a companion who could help. It is not that simple. I have seen patients who feel enormous reduction of agoraphobia being with an infant who would not be able to help, and some people use pets as companions. These patients realize that their companions would be useless in a time of crisis; nevertheless they feel far more comfortable being with an infant or a pet than being alone.

When I consider that the symptoms of agoraphobia relate to territoriality and companions it suggests some sort of tribal need. It would be of survival value to have a keen sense of how to avoid danger. Having an instinct that one has wandered into the territory of an enemy tribe or into the territory of dangerous animals would certainly have been "bred" into us if Darwin's theory of survival of the fittest were applicable. Similarly, in primitive times there must have been strength in numbers and staying with the tribe certainly would have been another trait that facilitated survival. Territorial concerns and tribal support remain important to this day and agoraphobia is an exaggeration of these inherent behaviors.

Agoraphobia is generally agreed to be the most insidious and complex symptom of panic disorder. It is actually less common for a person to feel "afraid' of going out than it is for them to talk themselves out of going somewhere ("I really don't like that restaurant very much..." or, "those people aren't really my friends anyway") and later to berate themselves for staying at home. The corollary is that confusion develops in which the person is unable to tell where they do and don't really want to go.

Posted March 2000 to the PDI bulletin board by Notsofast
This is so hard to explain because I don't understand it or know where the hesitancy comes from to do the things I used to do. I can run to town to get my son some necessities he needs but can't get myself to go buy myself a pair of shoes. I run the dog to the vet with no problem. The panic mode doesn't seem to enter into anything I want to do for my family. It seems like my brain doesn't have the want or desire to do simple or big things for myself.

This post clearly describes the experience of agoraphobia. This person realizes that they have an abnormal lack of desire to do activities of self-care but responsibility to others is intact. The unhappiness that surrounds this sort of behavior is often confused with depression. The patient needs to learn to have insight into when they are talking themselves out of going somewhere or doing something. Awareness of these behaviors can take a lot of effort but it is worthwhile. I usually advise patients to go to all social events and dates that they are invited to for a period of time, and then they can develop is a basis to compare which events are enjoyable and which are not.

Posted July 1998 to the PDI bulletin board by Fearpower
I was looking forward to going to my daughter's high school graduation. That night I got all dressed and ready to go, but just as I was reaching for the doorknob to go out the front door, I felt paralyzed. I couldn't go out the door, but I couldn't turn around either.

This sort of paralysis is a part of anxiety. Some patients find that they are unable to get out of a chair or to move at all in the face of the deadline of a social obligation. It is important to avoid the "social disfiguration" and isolation that results from constantly

47

declining invitations. If you do accept an invitation, do not cancel out, especially at the last moment. Many people with agoraphobia make plans to go to an event, get dressed and ready to go only to freeze at the last minute. Sometimes, as in the above post, this happens with their hand on the doorknob ready to go out. Socially, you are far better off declining an invitation than you are canceling your plans.

Chapter VIII: Anticipation

Anticipation is one of the most important and least understood features of panic disorder. In, <u>The Expression of the Emotions in Man and the Animals,</u> Darwin writes:

> *"When we direct our whole attention to any one sense, its acuteness is increased; and the continued habit of close attention, as with blind people to that of hearing, and with the blind and deaf to that of touch, appears to improve the sense in question permanently. There is, also, some reason to believe, judging from the capacities of different races of man, that the effects are inherited. Turning to ordinary sensations, it is well known that pain is increased by attending to it; and Sir B. Brodie goes so far as to believe that pain may be felt in any part of the body to which attention is closely drawn. Sir H. Holland also remarks that we become not only conscious of the existence of a part subjected to concentrated attention, but we experience in it various odd sensations. as of weight, heat, cold, tingling, or itching."*

If one starts to pay close attention to how our head feels, then one tends to feel headache. If one focuses on the heart, then one will tend to increasingly feel the intensity of the heartbeat. To focus on an area of the body can lead to the perception of unpleasant sensations from that part of the body.

Anticipation involves an intense degree of attention to bodily sensations. Anticipation of a symptom brings it on to a limited extent. For example, patients who have a *gran mal* seizure disorder may anticipate the possibility of having a seizure and this in turn may induce them to have shaking of the extremities that simulates an actual seizure. The person with a severe shellfish or peanut allergy who is mistaken about perhaps having ingested these foods and anticipates an allergic reaction can develop hives or wheezing. Anticipation of breathing difficulties can induce asthma in asthmatics. A person who has any sort of episodic illness can develop a similar condition of lesser intensity—anticipation based mirror image of the original symptom.

While this is a general principle in medicine it has been poorly studied and poorly documented. On the other hand, panic disorder patients have little difficulty in understanding that they experience this phenomenon. Once the subject of anticipation -induced panic attacks is brought up, patients readily identify the experience in themselves.

Although anticipation-induced panic attacks are not directly discussed in the *DSM IV*, the *DSM IV* definition includes the concept that a person must "worry about the significance of the attacks". Worry constitutes the sort of anticipation that brings on some of the symptoms of a panic attack. My patients can almost always realize that they are bringing on some of their own symptoms through anticipation. Anticipation is mental, yet the symptoms are as physical as problems with the head, heart, lungs and gut, as well as other organs. An observant person will realize that thinking about the panic attack symptoms creates them. Yet the experience is still seen as totally physical.

Patients often appear in my office having been told by a their doctor that their symptom is imaginary or fabricated—"all in your head." This means little to a patient who has had the experience of a clearly physical event. They are not fabricating their experience. They are puzzled by their experience but understand immediately that the anticipation of symptoms has been causing limited panic attacks.

Case study, Paul S.
A 49-year-old man presented with panic attacks that started after he had cardiac arrhythmia. A month before he developed

51

spontaneous atrial fibrillation. He felt his heart race out of control. As his blood pressure fell he became faint and fell to the ground. He was taken to the emergency room where a cardiologist injected him with a drug that restored his usual heart rhythm. Several days later he experienced the exact same symptoms and went back to the emergency room. This time he was told that his heart was normal

Over the next two weeks he returned three times for these same sensations only to be told that he had a normal heart rhythm and that he was having panic attacks. In consultation it emerged that the episode of atrial fibrillation was very frightening. When he was hungry or fatigued the sensation was similar to the beginning of the frightening experience he had felt when he had the atrial fibrillation. He realized within the first visit that when he was cued with the usual discomfort of fatigue or hunger he had anticipated atrial fibrillation and in his anxiety he induced rapid heart rate and a sensation of faintness. With psychotherapy he was able to recognize his symptoms as anticipatory and was able to avoid further panic attacks.

I think that "anticipation disorder" might be a better name for this condition than panic disorder. The symptoms that result from anticipation are a major part of the condition. The experience of anticipation-based symptoms is not necessarily anxiety based. A person can have what first appears to be appropriate concern for their health that inadvertently becomes the problem. Understandably this leads to even greater concern and even more symptoms. A vicious cycle develops. Ultimately the only way out of this sort of vicious cycle is to have a firm conviction that the physical sensation may be uncomfortable but is not dangerous. This conviction allows a person to focus attention elsewhere until the sensation passes.

The effects of anticipation are neurologically profound and not limited to anxiety. Essential tremor is a disorder of anticipation. Tremor is only present when the person anticipates that someone will be observing them while doing an action that requires some precision, such as carrying a cup of coffee or signing a check. It is the anticipation that the coffee will be spilled or that a signature will be unreadable that precipitates the tremor. If people with essential tremor can convince themselves that, for example, it doesn't matter at all what their signature looks like then they may be able to sign a check without tremor. Essential tremor and panic disorder can sometimes be found in the same patients. It may be that the common feature in both conditions is a heightened sensitivity to anticipation.

Chapter IX: Anger—the Sidecar of Panic

Posted to the PDI bulletin board May 1997 by Lori
Living with panic disorder since I was a small child has left me with so much anger. For me and many others this anger is just as much a symptom and a problem of panic disorder as is the agoraphobia and the "fear from nowhere". Does anyone understand how hard we fight to just be a part of society? How am I supposed to live with or deal with the anger, which is my shadow every day when I wake up? There are no medications that will take away the anger. The medication only covers the anger up. Why can't society understand? Why can't doctors understand?

Anger is both a result of the frustrating experience of panic disorder as well as a symptom of panic disorder itself. It is average for people with panic disorder to experience a lot of anger. When you feel angry and irritable more easily than other people, dealing with society is difficult.

When a person feels anger they want to do something about it. A sense emerges that anxiety is an abscess of the emotions and that if the built up pressure can be released then it will feel better. An urge to act on the anger to get rid of it is a part of anger itself.

Panic disorder has at least as high a suicide rate as depression, some say even higher. I suspect that anger plays a major role in this.

Suicide is an angry act, the final rejection of all of life and family. For a group of people who are worried about being sick and dying it would seem odd that they would go ahead and attempt suicide. Certainly it is not being attempted when the person is on the way to the ER with chest pain. Suicide in panic disorder is an impulsive act of anger.

Posted January 2001 to the PDI bulletin board by Tigger
The seething anger and resentment that are part of my illness are not normal. Medication may not cure anger, but it makes a difference. Since I started medicine three years ago, my perspective on life and life's events has changed dramatically. I still get angry. I still have bad days, etc. My anger isn't out of control. It doesn't possess me. My attitude and emotions are healthier.

This person describes a "seething anger and resentment" that is not normal. Elizabeth Kubler Ross said that real anger only should last about ten seconds. Some people choose to carry a chip on their shoulder, but the person with panic disorder finds that their anger doesn't seem to pass through them. Patients often remark that they sometimes find themselves intensely angry over events that happened decades ago. When they think about these long ago events, usually having been humiliated or offended by someone, they feel intense and fresh anger as if the incident had just occurred. The anger persists

long past the time that it has any significance at all.

Posted to the PDI bulletin board February 2002 by Incognito
I can relate! I am a control person and when you have panic
anxiety disorder you lose control when the attacks hit. I am very
angry at what this illness has done to my nursing career and to my
life as a wife and mother. My anger gets in the way of me seeing
things in their proper prospective. But on the other hand it allows me
to achieve my optimum level of functioning with this disorder. I too
have also been on the receiving end of the comments, "Oh Get A
Grip." Hmmm...if those people could only live in my body for 24
hours and feel what I feel they would know what it is like.

The above person realizes that their anger is distorted and not

always appropriate, however she knows that if she should pause

during her anger to look at it more closely, she would feel the cold,

nameless fear of anxiety that is far more uncomfortable. She also

notes that of the range of options she has when she feels this

discomfort, anger is the most functional.

Anger does express dissatisfaction, and many people are not

offended by an angry person and instead see suffering and have the

desire to help. Unfortunately a person can't get away with this 24

hours a day. For many people with panic disorder the day is a series of hurdles to be overcome. The effort expended in anger or fear, on what seems insignificant to others, is exhausting.

When you do exhaust yourself, if nobody appreciates the effort, this can be very anger provoking. After all of the will power and energy consumed, it is frustrating to hear others say, "See, we told you it was no big deal."

Anger does not get released when you hit a dummy with a stick or otherwise seek catharsis. Losing or expressing one's temper does not lead to greater calmness. You can't eliminate it, but if you can be aware of it, you can control it at least to the point where it does your life no damage. It is possible to diffuse anger with humor or spiritual forgiveness but this takes acknowledging the anger without feeling ashamed.

Certainly anger is a feature of panic disorder and one seldom addressed as a primary symptom. Anger can occur as a constant simmering symptom with a seemingly rational basis or as a discrete seemingly irrational episode in the form of a panic attack. What these posts and clinical experience suggest is that the abnormal anger is recognizable to the person experiencing it and therefore something

that can be potentially controlled.

Chapter X: Sleep

Insomnia is not a part of the *DSM IV* criterion, but bears special mention as a very significant aspect of panic disorder. Not all patients will have sleep disturbances but this is very common in panic disorder. Often lack of sleep seems to precede clusters of panic attacks by a few days or weeks.

Posted by to the PDI bulletin board October 2002 by JK
The first thing that happens is I start to sleep poorly. This poor sleep causes me to feel irritable, fatigued and less able to cope with things. If I continue to loose sleep, this causes a cascade effect, where I feel worse and worse, and start to worry about feeling worse. The additional worry makes it even harder to sleep, which makes me even more anxious and exhausted.

Most of the patients that I see with panic disorder have significant problems falling asleep or staying asleep. They tell me that although they may feel exhausted, when they lie down to go to sleep they paradoxically feel heightened alertness or may feel a startle response just as they start to relax. This is frustrating and patients can grow to dread the sleep experience. Some become angry at the inability to sleep and once angry, sleep is almost impossible. Often patients become preoccupied with lack of sleep because they feel that lack of sleep leads to panic attacks. Fear of sleeping poorly can cause insomnia. Patients argue over whether poor sleep leads to panic or whether it is the other way around. Anticipation related sleep disturbance aside, it is probably the same biological factors related to stress that causes *both* panic attacks and insomnia.

Patients can sometimes anticipate that they will have problems sleeping, and this can actually *cause* problems with sleeping. Worry concerning whether or not falling asleep will be prompt will in itself keep a patient awake. If a patient gets angry at himself for not sleeping then insomnia is almost guaranteed. It is important that patients accept that sometimes they will not sleep well and that they will sometimes feel fatigue. Fatigue is uncomfortable but it is temporary. When a person gets tired enough they will eventually fall asleep.

Anticipation of insomnia aside, sleep has a special role in panic disorder. Panic disorder overlaps with the sleep disorder narcolepsy in the symptoms of daytime drowsiness, hypnagogic hallucinations and sleep paralysis.

Hypnagogic hallucination is a state in which the person is consciously awake but the brain is dreaming. It usually lasts about five to ten minutes and then resolves spontaneously. The person can move freely and look around the room, but the subjective experience is that of the dream state. The person will feel awake and have their eyes open but will "see" that which they are dreaming and not what is real. This is very frightening.

Sleep paralysis is a state in which the person is consciously awake but has no control over the voluntary muscles. This is also frightening. The person wants to call for help but cannot. Again this usually lasts for about 5 to 10 minutes at the most and then resolves. When the person is able to speak again and tries to describe the experience to others, they usually tell the person that it was all a dream. Sleep paralysis is also fairly common in people who do not have panic disorder. Sleep paralysis and hypnagogic hallucinations are most common in childhood, before panic attacks and panic disorder emerge in the full syndrome.

Cataplexy is the other symptom of narcolepsy, in which a person collapses into the ground when they experience emotional excitement. Cataplexy does not happen in panic disorder.

Patients with panic disorder often report that they are unable to sleep if they get overtired or over stimulated before bedtime. Some patients find that they require a long period of relaxation before they can actually fall asleep.

Posted to the PDI bulletin board January 1999 by Cindy
It's not fair! I work with my husband, John, in the same office doing the same work. We run a series of small businesses and sometimes the pressure can get pretty intense and we end up working late into the evening. At the end of the day John and I are both exhausted, but when he is exhausted he flops down on the bed and starts snoring. As tired as I am I just can't fall asleep."

Panic attacks and panic anxiety tend to occur after a period of stress, at a time of rest, often waking people up at night. In patients like Cindy the same stimulating biochemical factors that cause nocturnal panic attacks are affecting them before falling asleep. Panic disorder patients tend to do better with a regular schedule for daytime activity allowing several hours to relax before bedtime.

Chapter XI: Interattack Worry and Hypochondriacal Thinking

In between panic attacks people with panic disorder tend to experience excessive worry. Patients worry most about whether they have physical diseases and they worry about when the next panic attack is going to happen.

Posted to the PDI bulletin board July 1998 by Donna M
No, I don't think I was ever happy between attacks. How can you be when you are waiting for another one to happen? You live your life in total apprehension. Sometimes I think that the attack is not as bad as the waiting for one. At least when you have an attack you know it will end (at least you HOPE it will:-) When I feel good between attacks I keep thinking, "why can't I feel this good everyday?" So you really never stop thinking about your condition even when the symptoms are not there. It's like waiting for the rug to be pulled out from under you again.

The other major problem between attacks is persistent concerns that physical sensations represent serious medical conditions. To some extent this is physician-induced. When medical doctors do not know what a particular symptom represents, they tend to be vague, order lots of anxiety provoking tests, and refer to other specialists who are often vague as well. Even if all of the tests are normal, physicians do not have good tools with which to describe normality. They don't tend to be reassuring. They are almost never completely sure that everything is normal. Sometimes this can go to an extreme where the patient becomes convinced that the doctors are holding back information about cancer or other serious medical illness. Everyone must live with a certain amount of physical discomfort or sensations that are unusual but the person with panic disorder has the tendency to worry about whether this might represent potentially fatal illness.

Beyond the fear of another attack or the fear of medical illness, the tendency to ask "what if" and anticipate the worst possible outcome of any experience is quite common. A stroll in the park leads to worry about a mugging or abduction. A headache leads to fear of a brain tumor. Buying a new car or a new house brings up fears of bankruptcy. These fears tend to occur even in the absence of a panic attack. Some people may interpret this trait as worry, negativity or depression, but to the patient this may just seem like necessary preparation.

The experience of "what if" thinking is a normal part of everyone's life. Before going out in the morning most of us check the weather. We need to determine whether or not it might rain and then to decide, perhaps, to carry an umbrella. This is a form of "what if" thinking. It is truly subjective as to where appropriate concern ends and worry begins.

Anxious worry almost always involves "what if" thinking. Worry involves expectation and anticipation that future events will be unpleasant, threatening or dangerous. Anticipation and evaluation of the future is necessary in order to make and carry out plans for the future. The difference between anxiety and concern can be subtle. People with anxiety need to develop insight into whether or not they tend to be overly concerned about negative consequences and potential danger. With practice this tendency can be altered.

Chapter XII: The Biology of Panic Disorder

The fear response, on a psychological and somatic basis, is "hard-wired" into the brain for basic survival purposes. Understanding some of the basics of the fear response provides an understanding of anxiety. Response to perceived threat has a number of components involving preparation for defense: autonomic sympathetic nervous system arousal, diminution of the sense of pain, potentiation of reflexes as well as a host of endocrine and other changes that prepare a person to optimally deal with threat. The response needs to be rapid and automatic under emergency circumstances and slower and well thought out under other circumstances.

A simplified anatomy of the fear response is as follows. Sensory cues first pass through the memory circuits of the deeper centers of the brain, called the hippocampus and amygdala. This triggers emotional memory of prior trauma eliciting a conditioned avoidance response. Under usual circumstances this is beneficial in preventing injury. The deeper centers of the brain connect to the prefrontal cortex to facilitate intellectual control of the fear response. The cortex can alter the effects of the conditioned response, but the original imprint of the memory still exists in the amygdala.

Eliminating the original imprint of memory is unlikely. If a person is becomes less sensitive to cued fear responses it is because they have learned a new context in which to understand the cue. For example, if a person were to have had a panic attack while eating at a certain restaurant while eating steak, they would tend to avoid this restaurant in the future. If they were to learn a new context, such as eating fish at this same restaurant, this could be enough of a change of context to allow dining at the restaurant.

During times of perceived intense threat the control shifts from the thinking cortex of the brain to the more primitive centers of the brain, the hippocampus and amygdala. Freud clinically noted this activation of the more primitive aspects of the brain under stress and called it "regression in the service of the ego." Output from the hippocampus to other parts of the brain results in a variety of neurological actions. Connections to the hypothalamus cause sympathetic nervous system activation. Examples of this include speeding of the heart rate or breathing rate. Connections to the vagus nucleus cause parasympathetic activation. Examples of this include drop of blood pressure, fainting or diarrhea. Outputs to other brain locations may cause hyperventilation, alarm and vigilance, fear of death or hormonal changes.

This model helps to explain the role of therapy in panic disorder. Working on strengthening the thinking aspects of experiencing stress can help to prevent the more primitive parts of the brain from being triggered. If you begin to feel fear and then become intensely frightened of an attack, then this can shut down the thinking related aspects of fear control. On the other hand, the person who starts to feel some anxiety and thinks, "Oh, this has happened before, it will pass soon" is going to be able to have a greater degree of control. One can choose to control emotional and interpersonal responses to a situation, but complete control may not always be possible.

Some people will be able to control panic attacks through cognitive processes, but others will find the nervous system simply too sensitive to maintain control of the more primitive parts of the brain through cognitive strengthening. In such people, medication can be of enormous benefit.

While the anatomy of fear has been worked out, the full biology of panic attacks and panic disorder remains speculative. The behavioral model of panic disorder explains panic attacks as intense anxiety responses to thoughts and normal bodily sensations. This is a reasonable explanation for some panic attacks, particularly attacks that are induced by anticipation. For many patients with panic disorder the symptoms of panic attacks come on abruptly, as if a switch was turned on. The physical symptoms are felt before the anxiety.

Patients describe their panic attacks as a "sudden surge of adrenalin." Subjectively it feels as if the fight or flight reflex has been triggered, but no adrenalin has been found to be released during panic attacks. If adrenalin is infused into a person with panic disorder it does not cause a panic attack. There are other substances that can be infused that will cause a panic attack, but this does not mean that these substances are *the* cause of panic disorder. Infusion of lactate is probably the best-known substance that may cause panic attacks.

Other substances that also cause panic attacks include the drug yohimbine, cholecystokinin and inhaled carbon dioxide. Infusion studies have been of great value in the study of panic disorder, but no infused agent can be considered the "cause" of panic disorder. Many hormones and neurotransmitters are involved in the stress response, however no single neurotransmitter or hormone is the "cause" of panic disorder. In particular panic disorder is not a disorder of serotonin deficiency.

While areas of the brain such as the amygdala and hippocampus are known to be involved in the fear or alarm response, it is really speculative as to what the role of these centers may be in panic disorder.

Sometimes people try to work backwards from the drugs that treat panic disorder to figure out a neurological basis. Certainly drugs that enhance the brain chemicals GABA and serotonin can help panic disorder, but to say that panic disorder is a serotonin or GABA deficiency is a lot like saying that arthritis is an aspirin deficiency. The bottom line is that the biology of panic disorder is an area of research study but that no comprehensive explanation for it has been established at this time.

The nerve cells that control brain activity, regulate the heart, keep us breathing and permeate almost every aspect of our body's conscious and unconscious activities, function by conducting electricity. When a nerve is stimulated electricity is conducted along the cell membrane in discrete units called action potentials. The more a nerve is provoked, the greater the number of action potentials that travel down its cellular membrane. One nerve cell normally connects to many other nerve cells. In this way, the electric activity of nerve cells act in a complex and highly connected arrangement, called a neural network.

Under experimental conditions neuroscientists have found that at moderate levels of electrical stimulation the neural network conducts a proportionate degree of electric activity. When excessively stimulated, the nerves in the network begin to fire at greatly enhanced frequencies out of proportion to stimulation. Electrical activity may continue to fire at an excessive rate even after the electrical stimulation is over. The more a neural network is stressed, the more sensitive it becomes to subsequent stimulation. In neurophysiology this enhanced sensitivity is referred to as hysteresis (no relationship to hysteria).

If the nervous system is stressed enough it can get "stuck" responding to a low level of stress as if it were responding to a higher level of stress. Panic attacks are generally experienced as an inappropriate stress response. Hysteresis in neural systems may be a fundamental component of panic attacks.

This model suggests that when the nervous system is overtaxed, a treatment that dampens the ability of nerve cells to react to stimuli is needed. This is exactly what anticonvulsants do. In fact, many anticonvulsants do show beneficial effects on panic disorder. Coincidentally panic disorder patients show a higher incidence of seizure disorder. The benzodiazepines (BDZs), Valium-like drugs, act to reduce nervous electrical activity and also have strong anticonvulsive properties. Panic attacks and seizures have a lot of similarities. Both are episodic, unexpected, occur during sleep and represent disproportionate nervous system activity.

The concept of hysteresis suggests that one important goal of treatment is to get the nerves in the stress or early warning centers to stop overreacting. Theoretically this can be accomplished in a variety of ways. One way is to strengthen the cognitive, thinking, part of the brain to modulate the alarm centers. Another way would be to use a medication that reduces the ability of cell membranes to conduct electricity. Clinically the use of BDZs seems to be able to reverse the hysteresis effect and subsequently restore a more normal response to stress that persists after the BDZs are stopped. The BDZs may be able to reset the stress response.

I think that the concept of hysteresis is a good explanation for what is happening in panic disorder. It is as if the alarm system and other aspects of the nervous system have been overtaxed and are now overreacting to trivial stressors. Single or multiple neurotransmitter theories are almost always retrospective and based on observations that one or another drug seems helpful. Looking at the clinical manifestations of panic disorder it seems that the fundamental problem lies not in any one neurotransmitter but in an entire nervous system that is sensitive and prone to unprompted electrical activity.

The alarm centers of the brain are the early warning system of the nervous system and are expected to be most sensitive to stress or sensory stimuli. But in panic disorder I also see problems in peripheral nerves, outside of the central alarm system, and any or all aspects of the nervous system can be involved in panic disorder. Furthermore, panic disorder is not just a series of panic attacks with normal health in between attacks. The myriad of symptoms between attacks also suggests that this is a whole nervous system phenomenon and not just an abnormal alarm system.

Chapter XIII: Medical Evaluation

The basic symptoms of panic disorder are similar to symptoms found in other medical and psychiatric conditions. For this reason, a patient with panic disorder generally needs a careful medical and psychiatric evaluation. Panic attacks can also be a nonspecific symptom of a medical illness anywhere in the body. Medical evaluation needs to screen for general health problems and for specific medical problems that may present as panic attacks. Medical evaluation involves general screening that is applicable to all patients, and also specific evaluations relevant to the symptoms of each patient. Medical conditions can both mimic panic disorder and contribute to panic disorder.

Senior citizens deserve special attention. Panic disorder tends to be a condition that becomes clinically significant in the late teens or early 20's. New onset of panic attacks in a person over 60 is always alarming and is much likelier to be a primary medical condition. It requires an intensive medical evaluation. I have seen panic attacks as the presenting symptom of cancer. Often older people have a combination of physical and psychological factors that cause panic attacks. So, even if a person is under a great deal of stress and the development of panic attacks seems to be an understandable response, in this population a very thorough medical workup needs to be done in addition to treatment.

Increasingly panic disorder is being diagnosed with no medical evaluation at all. Physicians often feel that panic disorder can be clinically diagnosed based on symptoms alone. Much of the time the tests that are ordered do not elicit any physical illness. On the other hand, a small percentage of patients will prove to have a primary medical illness causing panic attacks or a medical problem that is contributing to the panic disorder. Because the experience of panic disorder is most often that of a medical illness, it is also therapeutic for the patient to have a thorough physical examination with appropriate laboratory testing. Knowing that no medical illness is present allows a patient to better tolerate the discomfort of the condition.

Patients may have a fear that they are going crazy. The good news is that with this illness, when you think that you are losing your mind you are really OK. Currently family practitioners often elect to treat panic disorder without a psychiatric consultation. Some family physicians and internal medicine specialists are fairly good psychiatric diagnosticians, however my opinion is that the severity and chronicity of panic disorder mandates a careful psychiatric examination. The treating psychiatrist should make sure that the patient has a good medical examination and the family physician make sure that the patient has had a psychiatric consultation.

The Ambiguity of the Medical Evaluation

Patients are commonly ambivalent about medical workups. Panic disorder is often perceived as a physical problem and patients want to find out what that problem is. At the same time they are afraid that a severe, terminal illness will be found. Furthermore, a negative medical evaluation may not be sufficient to ease fears that a physical problem is really the root of the problem. This is because the medical evaluation is not as scientifically precise as one would imagine. Medical evaluation can be quite precise in its ability to identify life-threatening diseases. It is not nearly so precise in its ability to identify or rule out less serious illness. Often the results of

81

examination are ambiguous and lead to further tests and further specialty evaluation.

For example, seizure disorder needs to be considered as a possible cause for panic attacks. The test for seizure disorder is the EEG (electroencephalogram), which looks at the electrical activity at the surface of the brain. Many people who have seizure disorder will not show abnormalities on EEG. Clinical findings combined with EEG usually lead the clinician to a diagnosis. Ultimately this sort of diagnosis is a judgment call. So if you have an EEG that is negative, but still suspect that you have a problem with seizures, you cannot be sure that a seizure disorder is not present.

For the anxious individual this sort of uncertainty can be intolerable. Patients who are anxious may influence the clinical judgment of a physician through their anxiety. The clinical judgment of a doctor is always influenced by the degree of distress that the patient shows. And clinical judgment is highly subjective.

Case Study—This must be a tumor
Jill, a 51-year-old advertising executive with a long history of anxiety, began to notice that she could hear her heart beat in her left ear. Alarmed by this she went to her family physician for an evaluation. Her doctor was unable to find anything wrong on his

examination. He suggested that she get some rest and if she was not better in a month he could order some tests.

Highly concerned, Jill asked what kinds of tests was he thinking of, what sort of disease could it be? Why not order them now? Feeling that a more careful evaluation required a specialist, he referred Jill to an Ear Nose and Throat specialist.

Two weeks later when she saw the ENT specialist Jill was even more worried. The pulsatile sound now seemed more frequent and at times she felt dizzy. The ENT doctor ordered a magnetic resonance angiogram and a CT scan of the inner ear, both of which were normal. His exam was normal also. Certain that the problem was a tumor in her ear, she asked, "Is it possible that this could be a tumor in my ear?"

He replied, "I don't think so, very unlikely."

"But is it possible?"

"It would be very rare, but a small glomus tumor of the middle ear might be too small to show up on an studies but still cause a pulsatile sound...unlikely." He looked into her ear again. This time he was less certain about what he had seen. He thought he might have seen a slight bluish tinge to the eardrum. Uncertain because of his lack of expertise with this uncommon problem, he referred her to a university specialty center that had more experience with this.

Over the next few weeks, waiting for the next evaluation, Jill could hardly sleep. Not only did she seem to hear her pulse in her left ear, but it also seemed to hurt, as if a tumor was growing and putting pressure on her ear. Her dizziness was worse and she felt certain that she must have a glomus tumor. Her anxiety heightened when she read on the Internet that she was at the peak age for a glomus tumor of the middle ear.

The specialist at the university had seen many glomus tumors and reassured Jill that he found no evidence whatsoever for a glomus tumor. Still suspicious of a possible undiagnosed medical problem Jill finally decided that she would have to trust the doctors' opinions that this was just not a tumor. After the examination it seemed that the pulsatile sound was less and it did not seem to hurt. The symptom gradually went away completely over the next few weeks.

In Jill's case, she had a fairly common symptom of anxiety. Through her zeal to have a thorough evaluation she ended up with more anxiety, more symptoms and multiple physician consultations that did not satisfy her need for a definitive diagnosis. She suffered needlessly. The patient's anxiety can result in misdiagnosis, or microdiagnosis. Microdiagnosis is my term for when a doctor responds to the patient's anxiety and begins to order more and more tests that look at increasingly obscure aspects of physiology. Each test has a certain percentage of false positives and ambiguity in interpretation. Sooner or later a false positive or a set of ambiguous findings may lead to a diagnosis of a vague or obscure medical condition.

Of course there are always rare conditions that require careful diagnostic scrutiny, but in panic disorder it seems that either the medical system is spinning its wheels in an attempt to find an obscure disease or it is abdicating all responsibility to look for physical disease.

It is ultimately between the physician and the patient to decide the extent to which a given symptom should be medically evaluated. It is a process, part science, part intuition and part trust.

Chapter XIV: Screening Tests

I get a lot of e-mail from people with panic disorder who are unsure about what sort of laboratory studies and tests are needed. Because panic attacks can be a symptom of medical illness it is always wise to see your family physician for a check up when you are first diagnosed. No standardized medical evaluation exists however I do have general recommendations for screening tests that I consider to be useful.

Blood testing is a screen of general health. I suggest a complete blood count (CBC), thyroid studies, and a chemistry panel that usually includes general tests of liver function, kidney function, blood sugar and thyroid studies.

The CBC evaluates primarily for anemia, but also gives some information about possible B12, iron or folate deficiency by the size of the red blood cells. The white cell count gives a general idea about occult infection, or certain leukemias.

The chemistry panel is a very general screening test. The electrolytes (potassium, sodium, chloride and bicarbonate) as well as the blood urea nitrogen (BUN) and creatinine give a general assessment of the kidneys. Some measures of liver enzymes are typically included. In panic disorder it is not uncommon for the liver enzymes to be slightly elevated. This does not necessarily indicate liver disease. Very low elevations of the liver enzymes are a nonspecific finding in panic disorder, usually of no real significance. Cholesterol and triglycerides are usually included in a chemistry panel. Cholesterol is typically elevated in panic disorder. The cause of this is not known. Elevated cholesterol is a risk factor and not a disease. It is more of a problem in the context of a personal or family history of cardiac disease. Whether or not you choose to treat elevated cholesterol is something you need to work out with your own physician.

A fasting blood sugar is the basic screening for diabetes. Diabetes can cause various neurological problems that may be similar to panic disorder. Patients often feel weak, dizzy and hungry with panic disorder, symptoms that are common in panic disorder and hypoglycemia (low blood sugar). A single blood sugar level will not give a lot of information about hypoglycemia. One more specific test for this is a glucose tolerance test (GTT). In this test, the patient is given a high sugar beverage to drink and blood sugar is drawn every half hour or so for 3 to 5 hours. The rate of blood sugar decline as well as the absolute amount of decline is used to determine possible hypoglycemia. The test does not always correlate with symptoms. Some patients feel very hypoglycemic but have a normal GTT. Other patients may have a seriously abnormal GTT with no clinical symptoms of hypoglycemia. The GTT may actually induce mild hypoglycemia in some people and is not reliable. Another test useful to diagnose hypoglycemia is a blood sugar taken after a 24 hour fast.

Thyroid studies are important not only because thyroid disease can mimic panic disorder but also because people with panic disorder often develop thyroid disease. Thyroid studies are needed as a baseline and should be repeated every few years, especially when there is a flare up of panic attacks. Thyroid in the bloodstream comes in two types, T4 and T3. T4 is measured directly and T3 indirectly in a test called T3 uptake. The other major measure of thyroid is thyroid stimulating hormone (TSH), which is produced in the hypothalamus and stimulates the thyroid to produce T4 and T3. TSH is considered to be the most sensitive indicator of thyroid functioning. The lower the TSH values the more active the thyroid is. Most often the general public tends to associate elevated thyroid with panic disorder because thyroid tends to speed up the system. In my experience low thyroid has been far more common in panic disorder. There is some controversy about what constitutes low thyroid. The ranges of normal are thought to be too large and currently clinicians have started to treat patients in the low average range of thyroid functioning with thyroid replacement.

Optimal screening studies beyond blood testing should include an electroencephalogram, magnetic resonance image (MRI) or CT scan of the head and a Holter monitor study.

The electroencephalogram is used to evaluate for seizure disorders, which can sometimes appear similar to panic disorder. A panic attack comes on abruptly, seems involuntary, and usually lasts ten to twenty minutes much like a seizure. After the panic attack the person is drained of energy also similar to a seizure. Clinically the classic gran mal seizure is easily identified and almost never confused with a panic attack. Other types of seizures such as temporal lobe seizures and partial complex seizures may seem similar to panic attacks. It is common to find nonspecific temporal lobe abnormalities on EEG in panic disorder patients, which usually do not indicate a seizure disorder. Seizure disorders can be present with a normal EEG. For this reason, some neurologists may order multiple EEG studies. If a seizure disorder is strongly suspected it may be necessary for the patient to be put under telemetry video observation for 24 hours or more while EEG is being continuously monitored. The goal in this sort of study is to measure EEG while an attack is seen on video.

MRI or CT scans of the head are reasonable screening tests. The MRI imaging of the brain shows more detail than the CT scan, however the MRI involves being in a confined space for a half hour and many patients find this intolerable. Either test is appropriate as a screening tool. These tests look for any structural abnormality that could possibly be causing events similar to panic attacks. For example, a tumor on the nerve sheath of the inner ear, an acoustic neuroma, can cause dizziness. Increased pressure from any tumor can cause headache and neurological symptoms. Because panic attacks can be nonspecific symptoms, and headache is so common, it is a

good idea to obtain one of these examinations.

A Holter monitor is a machine that records EKG continuously

for a 24-hour period. A traditional EKG needs to be done to rule out

an acute cardiac event such as a heart attack. The EKG, however,

only looks at heart rhythm for a short period of time and often it is

taken after racing heart or chest pain is over. For patients with

recurrent episodes of racing heart, palpitations or chest pain it is

useful to have EKG monitored for a 24-hour period. This way, EKG

can be recorded while one of these events is occurring.

Chapter XV: Specific Medical Considerations

Sometimes the clinical picture suggests a medical condition that presents as panic attacks. Here are some that should be considered.

Drug related problems are common causes of panic attacks. Alcohol abuse is an extremely common cause of panic attacks. While alcohol abuse is common in people with panic disorder, people with alcohol abuse, with or without a history of panic disorder are prone to having alcohol-induced panic attacks. Alcohol-induced panic attacks usually occur several hours after heavy drinking. Marijuana is another drug that can induce panic attacks. Like alcohol, it can be used to alleviate anxiety but over time it tends to aggravate anxiety. Ecstasy users can also experience panic attacks after single dose or chronic use of the drug.

If hypertension is present, your family physician should consider the necessary workup for hypertension. Epinephrine secreting tumors, known as pheochromocytoma, are rare, but have been known to cause hypertension and simulate panic disorder. It might be appropriate to obtain a 24 hour urine sample to look for metabolites of epinephrine.

Gastroesophageal reflux and gastritis are very common in panic disorder. I do not usually order special studies for these problems unless they do not significantly improve with initial treatment. If medications are ineffective in treating the symptoms of heartburn then it may be reasonable to get an endoscopic examination of the stomach and esophagus.

Mitral valve prolapse is a fairly common finding in people with and without panic disorder. Most often mitral valve prolapse is asymptomatic. In this condition the mitral valve is large relative to the size of the heart. Because of this a leaflet of the valve puffs out causing the murmur. Because people with panic disorder have such a high incidence of chest pain, they often get echocardiograms that shows mitral valve prolapse. It is usually not symptomatic and requires no treatment.

Panic disorder is often worse during the premenstrual period. Some women do measure estrogen, progesterone and testosterone levels with the idea that an imbalance in these hormones is a part of their problem. These can be measured from the blood or saliva. My clinical experience is that there is no consistent hormonal imbalance that aggravates panic disorder. Some women feel better when they take extra estrogen and others with progesterone or testosterone, however hormones make some women feel worse. Finding the potentially helpful hormones is a lengthy process of trial and error. It is usually not worthwhile to work with these hormones, but some women have found hormone these treatments to be valuable. Given the potential risks of hormone replacement therapies this sort of treatment approach should be provided under medical supervision.

On the Internet there is a lot of interest in what is described as subclinical adrenal exhaustion. Usually the sites that discuss this are selling diagnostic tests and supplements that are supposed to support adrenal function. This may one day prove to be significant, but so far I am not convinced that subclinical adrenal exhaustion is a valid clinical entity.

Excess adrenal steroid release, Cushing's Syndrome, and insufficient adrenal steroid release, Addison's Disease, both have clear cut physical symptoms that should alert the physician. In

Cushing's, patients typically have obesity of the stomach but not the extremities, hypertension, fractures and a peculiar type of bluish stretch marks. In Addison's disease patients show typical changes in skin pigmentation, low blood pressure and weight loss. When I am concerned about the possibility of these conditions I will order morning cortisol levels for basic screening. Cushing's Syndrome and Addison's disease are not common problems.

Acute intermittent porphyria is a rare inherited abnormality of the metabolism of hemoglobin. It presents as intense episodes of abdominal pain. Because of the lack of physical findings and its episodic nature, it may be mislabeled as panic disorder. Abdominal pain is often precipitated by a variety of medications. The test to evaluate for this condition is measurement of urinary porphobilinogens.

Lyme disease occasionally presents a clinical picture similar to panic disorder. Some patients develop neurological Lyme disease with sensitivity to light and touch and shifting neurological pain. The anxiety is secondary to the physical symptoms. Lyme disease is spread by a tick bite, and is preceded by a typical "bulls eye rash" at the site of the bite. Blood tests look for the presence of antibodies to the parasitic agent that causes Lyme disease. This test has a lot of false positives and false negatives and does not diagnose an active infection. The blood tests are used to confirm clinical suspicion.

Heavy metal toxicity such as mercury, antimony, arsenic and cadmium can present similar to panic disorder. If exposure to these agents is suspected, then it can be evaluated by either blood testing or hair analysis.

Head injury is an often-overlooked precipitant of anxiety and panic attacks. Symptoms may persist for months after a concussion even after other symptoms have resolved. The person need not have lost consciousness in order for head injury to cause longer lasting symptoms.

Toxic house mold (Stachybotrys, Pennicillium and Aspergillis) can be a cause of panic attacks. The mold itself can cause anxiety episodes. Also some people develop a conditioned avoidance response to the effects of the mold and will develop anxiety as they approach a house with mold.

Wheat gluten intolerance bears special mention. Gluten is a protein in wheat that is ubiquitous. Used in almost all of the vegetarian frozen foods to provide a "meat like" consistency and in most processed starches, we are saturated with gluten in our diets. Gluten is a psychoactive molecule and can cause a variety of psychiatric symptoms including panic attacks. Allergy testing can be done for antibodies to gluten, however antibodies to gluten need not be present for a person to be reacting to gluten. In its most extreme form gluten allergy causes a wasting of the lining of the small intestine with malabsorption and diarrhea known as celiac disease. People with celiac disease are quite ill. Gluten intolerance is associated with gastrointestinal complaints but presents with symptoms that are similar to anxiety. Restriction of wheat gluten from the diet is the best way to test for the effects of gluten. It only takes 3 to 5 days of dietary restriction to experience relief from gluten intolerance. It takes a bit of effort to eat a gluten free diet, but it is a reasonable test to screen for this potential cause or aggravation of panic disorder. Websites such as *celiac.com* can tell you which foods to avoid.

Chapter XVI: Psychiatric Evaluation

If you have panic disorder you should have an evaluation by a psychiatrist. However, you should know that the diagnoses of the *DSM IV* for disorders tend to overlap and are highly subjective. People are commonly given several of these descriptive diagnoses at a time but it does not necessarily mean that the patient really has several conditions in need of treatment. The current tendency is to give a patient as many labels as possible. Patients need to be aware that multiple labels can be put on the same set of symptoms. Psychiatric diagnosis has no definitive lab tests. Psychiatric diagnosis is standardized in a descriptive fashion, but psychiatric diagnosis itself tends to have a lot of room for subjective interpretation.

Given this disclaimer about diagnosis, psychiatric evaluation is the best way to establish your diagnosis and to set up an appropriate treatment plan. Some people prefer to have their medications prescribed by their family physician. Even if you are treated by your family physician it is a good idea to at least get a psychiatric consultation. Here are some psychiatric conditions that may overlap with panic disorder:

Depression: People with depression often have panic attacks. Conversely a portion of people with panic disorder will become significantly depressed. Many people with longstanding panic disorder will "wear out" from the experience and fatigue will seem similar to depression but lifts quickly when panic attacks stop. Because clusters of panic attacks are so distressing a *DSM IV* diagnosis of depression is often a valid description of a person's mood. It is common to see the diagnosis of panic disorder given along with major depressive disorder but for practical purposes they are describing the same set of clinical findings. There is a trend now for many prescribing physicians to look at panic disorder as another form of depression. Treatment for depression may be initiated simultaneously with or even in place of specific treatment for panic disorder. In my practice I treat the panic attacks first and then wait to see if the person is still depressed. Most of the patients who get good relief from panic attacks do not prove to be depressed.

Schizophrenia: Psychotic people find it an anxiety provoking experience. Panic attacks in the early stages of schizophrenia are common. Often people with panic disorder fear that they are going crazy. It is not typical for schizophrenic people to have insight into their delusions or irrational reasoning. In contrast, people with panic disorder commonly feel as if they are going insane or fear that they will go insane. Some patients do have both schizophrenia and panic disorder and in these cases the schizophrenia tends to dominate the clinical picture.

Obsessive-compulsive disorder (OCD): Repetitive thoughts and rituals characterize OCD. The interattack worry of panic disorder usually focuses on the same themes over and over (such as financial or health concerns). Worry about the same thing over and over is really the definition of anxiety and is present in panic disorder. By current psychiatric standards, which only require repetitive thoughts for the diagnosis of OCD, worry will almost always meets the diagnostic criterion for OCD. So it is extremely common for panic disorder patients to also be told that they have OCD. For me, this is not sufficient for a separate diagnosis of OCD. I require actual obsessive rituals such as hand washing, or checking and rechecking locks before I make a separate diagnosis of OCD. It is very common for psychiatrists to add OCD to the diagnosis of panic disorder based on repetitive worry alone. True OCD with rituals does overlap with panic disorder. People with primary OCD may have situational panic attacks when they are unable to perform a ritual. At other times panic attacks are in reaction to the experience of compulsive rituals that do not alleviate anxious concerns.

Generalized Anxiety Disorder (GAD): All people with worry meet the criterion for this vague and nonspecific condition. It is applied to people with panic disorder frequently. Usually it refers to a person who has a long history of worrying. I do not consider it useful to make a separate diagnosis of generalized anxiety disorder in anyone with panic disorder. Psychiatric evaluators often apply the diagnosis of GAD to people with panic disorder. This combination of diagnoses, on a practical level, does not indicate that the person is suffering from two distinct anxiety disorders.

Manic Depressive Illness (MDI, also known as bipolar disorder): Most people with panic disorder tend to have some degree of mood instability. In panic disorder it is common for people to be very happy when anxiety is not present and have a depressed mood when it is problematic. This can appear similar to a pathological mood swing, but is better viewed as the patient having more or less energy and enjoyment when panic disorder symptoms are absent or present. The usual mood swings of panic disorder are significantly milder than in bipolar disorder. However, in the psychiatric profession it is appropriate to note these mood swings with a separate diagnosis of bipolar disorder. Currently bipolar disorder is the single most common secondary diagnosis I see given to patients with panic disorder. If mood swings are mild I find it best not to prescribe a mood stabilizer. It only complicates matters to add in the side effects of the mood stabilizers when they are not necessary. On the other hand, it is important to be alert to clinically significant mood swings. The diagnosis is most clear when there has been an episode of mania. Some common symptoms of mania include euphoria with hypersexuality, excessive spending of money, poor judgment no need for sleep and rapid speech. Mania can progress to a point where the patient becomes highly irritable and begins to hallucinate. Some patients clearly have both panic disorder and bipolar disorder. I call this "manic panic" and it is one of the most severe forms of panic disorder that I see. In manic panic treatment needs to be for both the panic attacks and the mood swings. The patient needs to be closely monitored for suicide.

Chapter XVII: Psychopharmacology

If patients are having clusters of panic attacks or symptoms that are intolerably uncomfortable then the benefits of drug treatment clearly outweigh the risks. Otherwise careful consideration is needed before deciding on treatment with drugs, especially if it is going to be an ongoing treatment. Numerous studies have indicated that the long-term prognosis is better if drug therapies are avoided in favor of psychotherapy. It is not clear to me exactly why patients do better in the long term if they have not been prescribed drugs. It may be that the patients in these studies who did not need drugs had milder forms of panic disorder. Alternately it has been theorized that drugs can weaken a person's innate coping skills.

When placebo controlled studies are performed for drug treatments of panic disorder most show about a 50% placebo response rate. This data almost makes an argument for the use of placebo. Because of the high placebo response rates it is easy to show some improvement in panic disorder symptoms in an open clinical trial of almost any drug tested. Statistically you would expect improvement in about half the people in the trial. Of course, the people who are selling the drug pay for almost all of the clinical trials and this source of bias that should not be taken for granted. The large numbers of people with panic disorder constitute an enormous market for drugs. A large percentage of psychiatric medications are promoted for panic disorder, so this can get confusing.

Any drug with sedative properties is going to improve the subjective experience of anxiety to some extent. Sedative properties of drugs tend to wear off after short periods of time. Also, many of the psychotropic drugs that are sedating also have a high degree of dependency or other adverse effects. The risk/benefit ratio argues against using these agents. In my practice, if a BDZ fails to control panic attacks, I tend to re-evaluate my diagnosis or to consider psychotherapeutic techniques instead of moving to the next set of drugs. Many clinicians will opt to try one drug after the next in hope of finding one that works.

Psychopharmacology is a trial and error process, one that, at times, lacks common sense. Often when a patient goes to a psychiatrist or family doctor with a problem the doctor assumes that the patient is seeking a drug to treat the problem. The physician may not even think about whether a particular condition might do better with therapy alone. Patients are not always aware of this.

If the first pill doesn't work, then another will be tried on the next visit. There is no science that actually guides the physician accurately in clinical practice. The literature may provide guidelines for the use of a particular drug, but there are no guidelines for the starting and stopping of several different drugs, and little information on the many combinations of drugs being used.

What is lacking is a clinical understanding of the withdrawal effects and side effects of the drugs being prescribed. Whenever a drug prescribed for the nervous system is stopped withdrawal effects will occur. Whenever a new drug is started there will be some unwanted initiation effects and side effects. All too often a patient has intolerable side effects from a specific category of drug and when this is stopped and another drug of the same category is prescribed. The withdrawal effects and initiation side effects overlap when this happens. Psychopharmacology is often lacking plain common sense. Patients complain that doctors have stopped listening to their complaints about adverse effects and side effects. Doctors sometimes appear to be overly influenced by the information given to them by the pharmaceutical companies and under-influenced by what they observe in their patients.

So when starting on a drug there are usually some unwanted effects. When it is stopped you can usually expect some withdrawal symptoms. In the practice of psychopharmacology drugs are started and stopped at a fairly rapid clip, inducing side effects and withdrawal effects in the process. Over a few months of this sort of treatment the distinction between your original symptoms and the complications of the drugs prescribed becomes blurred. The next set of drugs prescribed may well be used primarily to treat the complications of prior drug administration and withdrawal.

Some mental illnesses are so debilitating and so disturbing that this style of medical practice is justified. But it still lacks a scientific foundation. Nothing will send a person with panic disorder into disability faster than prescribing and un-prescribing several drugs at once. With the high incidence of adverse reactions and allergies, people with panic disorder are highly vulnerable to the complications of psychotropic medications.

Panic disorder feels like a medical illness (and probably should be considered a medical rather than a psychiatric illness) so it is only natural to seek a drug, or external resource, that is going to cure it. Drug treatments are important aspects of dealing with panic disorder, but common sense needs to be used when undergoing drug treatment. Some aspects of psychopharmacology can make treatment more like quicksand than a life raft.

Treating Panic Disorder: Stop the Attacks

The single most important feature of treating panic disorder is to stop the panic attacks. Most people can tolerate an occasional panic attack. Even people who do not have panic disorder are likely to have an occasional panic attack. Isolated panic attacks usually do not require drug therapy. In many instances, beyond reassurance, they require no treatment at all. When panic attacks occur frequently then it is important to use a medication to stop the attacks.

When panic disorder is at its worst, panic attacks tend to occur in clusters on a daily basis or even more often. Sometimes a single panic attack can persist for days at a time, a state that I refer to as "status panicus". When this happens a person can become rapidly disabled and is so uncomfortable that they may attempt suicide. Sometimes it is almost as if the attacks feed on each other with each attack causing the next attack to occur with increasing frequency and intensity. Patients may end up going to the emergency room several days in a row. It is the clusters of attacks that bring most of the patients to my office. Stopping these clusters of attacks is the first order of business in treatment. The attacks are intensely uncomfortable. The longer the attacks are allowed to proceed with no treatment, the more secondary phobias and anticipatory anxiety develops. Doctors do not always focus on the importance of promptly stopping attacks when they initiate treatment.

Benzodiazepines

Use of a benzodiazepine (BDZ) is the single most effective way to stop clusters of panic attacks or status panicus. There are a large variety of BDZs on the market, however the three that I have found most effective are alprazolam (Xanax), clonazepam (Klonopin) and lorazepam (Ativan), in that order. While the mechanism of action is the same for all BDZs, patients may have individual preferences for one BDZ over another. While I prefer to initiate treatment with alprazolam, if a patient already has been prescribed clonazepam or lorazepam and feels that these are helping there is usually nothing to gain by a change to alprazolam.

The BDZs are the only drugs that will stop the attacks quickly. Additionally, they help to reduce panic-related reflux. BDZs can be used for very short periods of time, intermittently or continuously whereas the other drugs have no effect on reflux and tend to be used for indefinite periods of time. While BDZs are outstanding agents to halt panic attacks, they are not nearly as good at stopping the experience of worry. The typical "what if" sort of thinking and the consequences of anticipation are appreciably less responsive to BDZs.

As effective as BDZs are, many doctors are afraid of working with BDZs. This is particularly true of alprazolam (Xanax):

Posted to the PDI bulletin board January 2001 by James T
Why are MD's and Psychiatrists unwilling to prescribe Xanax for Panic Disorder? Some background info: I have had panic disorder and agoraphobia for over 30 years. The last 12 years have been almost completely panic-free due to my doctor prescribing Xanax 1mg. 3x daily. My doctor just retired so I have been in search of a new doctor. I was told by the last doctor that I saw that I should

NOT be taking Xanax and that I SHOULD be taking an SSRI! He prescribed just enough Xanax for me until I could see a psychiatrist at a local mental health clinic. The psychiatrist at the local mental health clinic said her policy and the policy of the mental health clinic is NO BENZOS! Now I ask you Dr. Shipko, seeing as how Xanax has worked so well for me what is their problem with prescribing it?

Thanks for your time,

I think the problem is lack of education. It is true that the BDZs are often inappropriately prescribed resulting in addiction with dosages spiraling out of control. They are frequently prescribed for the wrong medical conditions, in the wrong dosage, for the wrong duration and often with inadequate supervision. Physicians have been *warned of addiction* but often have not been *educated in the appropriate usage of the drug.* The result of this is that doctors often think of the BDZs *only* as drugs of abuse and not as drugs of enormous therapeutic value.

Of the BDZs my preference is alprazolam (Xanax). I prefer it for several reasons. I have extensive experience with Xanax and feel comfortable working with it. I find it to be the single most effective agent to stop panic attacks. It is less sedating than Ativan (lorazepam) or Klonopin (clonazepam). I find that Klonopin is often too sedating and causes a sort of drowsy depression in about 10% of the people who take it. Ativan is also more sedating than Xanax and is less effective for panic attacks. Of the three BDZs mentioned Ativan is the only one never approved by the FDA for the treatment of panic disorder. While all of the BDZs have the capability of reducing reflux, Xanax is the only drug that I personally have studied in this regard. Clinically I feel strongly that it is the best choice of agent for stopping panic attacks. It is rapid acting and has a short half-life, which allows me to fine tune the dosing. Some professionals think that, because of the short half life, Xanax is more dependency-forming than Ativan or Klonopin, however my experience is that all three of these drugs are equally dependency forming.

Recently a new formulation for Xanax has entered the market. It is called Xanax XR and is long acting and is supposed to only be taken once daily. Because this is so new I have no clinical experience with it. Chemically it is the same as Xanax and I would expect it to have clinical effects that are roughly the same as the standard Xanax.

Chapter XVIII: General Concepts in Working with BDZs

Panic disorder patients have a lot of anxiety about what they put into their bodies. If a patient is highly anxious about adverse reactions to BDZs I do not spend much effort trying to convince them that it is in their best interest to give it a try anyway. If a patient is anxious about adverse effects from the BDZs, then pure fear of the pill can cause a panic attack. Anxiety over having taken a BDZ can easily overwhelm the beneficial effect of the drug. If the patient is scared of taking a BDZ this fear can produce a panic attack. This sort of fear reaction will occur almost immediately after taking the BDZ. This is as opposed to biological adverse reactions that don't start for a half hour or more, until drug has time to get into the bloodstream. To the patient with a phobia against the medication it seems as if the BDZ is working in reverse.

Taking BDZs as needed for panic attacks is often ineffective. A typical panic attack lasts about 20 minutes, and it usually takes about that long for BDZs to get into the bloodstream. It takes about as much time for the BDZ to enter the bloodstream as it would for the attack to go away without any medication at all. Taking BDZs in this fashion minimally influences the course of the panic attack. This sort of prescribing sometimes leads to obsessive self-monitoring of emotional state, constantly questioning whether or not this could be a "Xanax moment."

On the other hand, telling the patient that they can take the BDZ when they have a panic attack can have beneficial psychological effects. Patients have the security of knowing that if panic anxiety is every truly out of all control, then they have a safety net. The very knowledge that they have an antipanic agent available is enough to reduce or eliminate many anticipation-induced attacks. This can be a valuable strategy for the patient with phobic or anticipation related situational panic attacks. Often such patients will carry around a BDZ for years and never actually take a tablet. This is an effective form of indirect use of BDZs.

Directly or indirectly BDZs work best as a preventative drug. They are most effective when taken at the same time each day with the goal being to prevent any further attacks. When treatment is initiated, it is usually sedating for about three days, but by the fourth day the sedative side effects wear off. Patients who have a great deal of insomnia and are exhausted may appreciate the sedative side effect. The goal is to use a dose that eliminates all panic attacks but is not sedating. I want to underscore that when I prescribe a BDZ my goal is to prevent *all* spontaneous panic attacks. A reduction in panic attack frequency is not enough. This still keeps the patient guessing when the next big attack is going to occur. For a good treatment result, the patient needs to feel secure that they are very unlikely to have a major spontaneous attack.

With a BDZ the full-blown out of the blue panic attack can be prevented, but other aspects of anxiety are less responsive to BDZs. Patients need to realize that anticipating a panic attack will bring on some limited symptoms of a panic attack and no drug will totally stop anticipation induced symptoms. However, once the uncued panic attacks have stopped then anticipation of future panic attacks is often much less of a problem.

Just like an earthquake, after the panic attacks have stopped, patients will have "aftershocks". These are brief periods of time in which the patient feels as if they might be having a panic attack or are experiencing some limited symptom attacks. In the absence of spontaneous panic attacks I have observed that my patients show considerable skill in adapting to the aftershocks and often are able to successfully extinguish these symptoms.

Education, self-regulation and tolerance of some anxiety symptoms are necessary components of BDZs treatment. Treatment is less than perfect if a BDZ is prescribed without a careful discussion of the role of anticipation in symptom formation.

Once the correct dosage is achieved hopefully no further uncued panic attacks will occur. This usually takes from two days to about two weeks. Some people find that they have no aftershocks but for most symptoms of worry and brief episodes of physical symptoms may still be present. Sometimes patients continue to feel as if a panic attack is about to start, but this feeling goes away after a while when the patient is sure that the spontaneous attacks are in remission. After the unexpected attacks have stopped, it is easier to tackle other aspects of the condition. As with any other medical treatment this is not going to work for everyone. Still, I consider the use of a BDZ with the goal of stopping spontaneous attacks as the best initial treatment strategy.

Duration of BDZ Treatment:

Some people will take only an occasional pill, others will be on a brief course of treatment and still others are going to do best using a BDZ on an ongoing basis. Panic disorder is often a chronic, recurrent condition. For this reason, I favor episodic treatment when the condition recurs. The BDZ is used to stop attacks and once the attacks have stopped, I begin to taper and stop the BDZ. Years ago I considered the BDZ treatment to be analogous to insulin in diabetics, where a deficiency required indefinite replacement. Now I have more of an antibiotic analogy in which the panic attacks are knocked out and the BDZ is withdrawn after a short course of treatment.

In panic disorder when clusters of attacks are happening there is a tendency for the nervous system to be fixed in a highly stressed state. I view the use of a BDZ as a means to permit the nervous system to reset to a state of lower stress. Patients can also learn to use BDZs strategically to prevent the occurrence of further panic attacks. While some people clearly do better with regular daily long term use of a BDZ, the majority of the patients I treat do best on a short course of a BDZ, just until the panic attacks have stopped.

Stopping the BDZ is discussed right at the time that it is first prescribed. Most of my patients have obtained information that tells them that the withdrawal from BDZs is worse than any other drug. If you are a BDZ addict this is true. If you are taking a BDZ as prescribed then withdrawal is uncomfortable, but so far none of my patients have had to miss work when they are stopping BDZ. Before I even prescribe a BDZ I warn patients that the goal of treatment is to take it until the nervous system is calmed, and then to stop it. Withdrawal symptoms are highly variable; some people have little or no withdrawal symptoms and some people have significant discomfort. The withdrawal is not nearly as bad as the panic disorder that it is treating and most patients consider this to be an acceptable trade off. Patients, surprisingly, are able to tolerate withdrawal symptoms even when they mimic panic anxiety. Because they know that what they are experiencing is withdrawal and not a relapse of anxiety, the symptoms are tolerable. The withdrawal experience is similar to the experience of anxiety but during proper discontinuation there is generally not a return of spontaneous panic attacks. Human beings are unpredictable. If by chance unexpected panic attacks do return, then the patient restarts the BDZ and the process can be repeated. It is uncommon, but if attacks return on tapering, it is reasonable to continue them for several months before considering tapering again. When patients report that they had panic attacks on stopping their BDZs, they are usually getting anxious about a withdrawal symptom. For this reason, careful education about what to expect during withdrawal is important. Withdrawal symptoms occur commonly even after fairly short courses of treatment. So-called rebound symptoms are just another name for withdrawal. Actual relapse after stopping BDZs is uncommon.

The tendency for the nervous system to become overstressed is not changed by treatment with a BDZ. After a successful treatment with a BDZ if the patient becomes overstressed, then clusters of attacks tend to recur. This tends to occur at a later date, but it tends not to occur immediately after successful treatment. Relapse after stopping medication is something that the patients are afraid of. It is important to confront this fear at the same time that the medication is first prescribed.

It appears to be safe to take BDZs on a long-term basis. Common reasons for a patient to require long-term treatment with BDZs are intense interattack symptoms such as palpitations, hyperventilation or heartburn. Patients who have had severe panic disorder that has persisted untreated for years are another category of patient who may do better on long-term continuous treatment. It is not easy to predict who is ultimately going to require long-term treatment so this also must be discussed with the patient before initiating treatment. For those who are taking BDZs long- term tolerance to the therapeutic effects does not usually occur over time. In some people there can be tolerance and the dose gradually increases. In this case it is best to taper and stop the BDZ before the dosage goes too high. Long-term use will ameliorate but not prevent clusters of panic attacks from occurring during periods of high stress. Patients who are on long-term BDZ regimens will need to transiently increase the dosage from time to time if panic clusters occur.

People often ask about whether alprazolam can cause "permanent brain damage." Some anecdotal reports have shown enlargement of the ventricles in people who have used BDZs for long periods of time, but to date, there is no clinical or research evidence that long term use of the BDZs causes brain damage. I have seen people on BDZs for over two decades with little or no side effects. Long-term use of BDZs is not associated with cancer and may reduce the risk of pancreatic cancer. Since panic disorder is associated with increased morbidity and mortality from cardiovascular causes it is possible (but never studied) that long term BDZ use may reduce this risk.

The literature says that the BDZs are cross-tolerant. In other words if you substitute one BDZ for another, you should not have withdrawal. My experience is that the BDZs seem to have a limited cross-tolerance. For example, one of my patients who was on clonazepam wanted to switch to alprazolam because of the depressive side effects. She was on 0.5 mg twice daily of clonazepam and we attempted to change to 0.5 mg of Xanax twice daily. This patient went into full withdrawal despite substituting alprazolam for clonazepam. Differences in the equivalency of the drugs can explain some discomfort but not a full withdrawal syndrome. My observation is that it is much easier to change from alprazolam to clonazepam or lorazepam than the reverse.

In an uncomplicated case of panic disorder the process of tapering BDZs begins about two or three weeks after the cessation of unexpected panic attacks. In some patients tapering begins within a month of the initial prescription and in others this may take up to a year or two. It is important that the patient feel comfortable with the idea of going off medication. If the patient is anxious about stopping medication, fearing relapse, then the result is usually an anticipation-driven relapse. Sometimes this takes months of reassurance before a patient feels confident enough to "risk" stopping medication. The withdrawal at a particular dosage after a few years does not seem to be much different than the withdrawal that occurs after a few months, so time is not critical as far as the withdrawal effects of BDZ. What is critical is the patient's frame of mind about stopping the BDZ. The placebo effect plays a major role in the experience of withdrawal. Just as the anxious expectations of the patient can overwhelm the beneficial effects of the BDZ on administration, the anxious expectations have a major effect on the experience of withdrawal. I wait until the patient feels comfortable with the idea of stopping BDZs because this makes the process far easier.

Chapter XIX: Prescribing Benzodiazepines

Before prescribing BDZs, it is necessary to inform the patient completely about all potential side effects. The major side effects are:

Idiosyncratic reactions. This is a type of disinhibition in which a person becomes angry or aggressive and may behave inappropriately. It will appear after the first dose and is a clear contraindication to taking any further doses. I have found that this is not common in panic disorder and tends to occur in nonpanic anxiety states treated with BDZs. If it does occur, then BDZs should be stopped completely. *Memory impairment.* This tends to be worse as people age. Problems with word finding are most common. Memory impairment is occasionally significant enough that BDZs must be stopped. Some people who have marked memory impairment as a result of their anxiety and feel that memory is actually better after taking BDZs. This is usually mild. Some people may not recognize their loss of memory.

Drowsiness. The first three or four days that patients take BDZs they can expect to feel sedated. After that time sedation is less of a problem. There is usually, but not always, at least some degree of sedation associated the use of BDZs even after the first few days. Studies have shown that BDZs given to people without anxiety interferes with driving. The effects of BDZs on the driving skills of people with panic disorder have never been studied. Many of my patients tell me that because their anxiety is reduced that they are better drivers. Certainly one should not drive if BDZs are causing drowsiness.

Dependency. Dependency is defined as the inability to stop a drug without experiencing withdrawal symptoms. This is probably the most consistent side effect. Most people who take BDZs on a regular basis for more than a few days are going to experience withdrawal symptoms. These symptoms are minimized when BDZs are stopped slowly. Withdrawal symptoms tend to last from a few days to a few weeks. The most common withdrawal symptoms are insomnia, tension headache, irritability, heightened sensitivity to sound and smell, muscle and skin pain, metallic taste, loss of appetite, diarrhea and a sense of shakiness. If BDZs are stopped too abruptly then seizures are possible. Once a patient is on a BDZ they should only stop them under physician supervision.

Rapid metabolism. I have seen people who seem to metabolize BDZs, particularly alprazolam much faster than would be expected. They get an hour or two of benefit and then quickly start to feel tremulous, irritable and anxious. When this happens the BDZ must be discontinued. The BDZs are not all metabolized via the same liver enzymes so changing to a different BDZ can solve this problem.

Read the label. I consider any problem that was not present before taking a drug that is present after taking a drug to be a side effect until proven otherwise. Sometimes the patient needs to stop the drug and then restart the drug to be sure that a specific symptom is actually a side effect. Outside of the side effects that I have described I generally do not find that patients are having a lot of other problems when taking BDZs. Still, any drug can cause a wide variety of side effects. Blurred vision, constipation, allergy, heightened appetite and sexual dysfunction are infrequent side effects that I have also observed.

BDZ Dosing

The starting dosage ranges of the BDZs are highly variable. For alprazolam or lorazepam a dose of about 0.5 mg three times a day is an average starting dose. Some people do best on half that dose and others on twice that dosage. Clonazepam should be taken twice daily. A common starting dose is 0.5 mg with some people, again, some people will take half that dose and others twice that dose.

I have seen different "equivalency" charts describing the relative potency of clonazepam, lorazepam and alprazolam. Because of differences that patients have to the effects of these drugs, the equivalency of the three drugs is irrelevant. For prescribing purposes the three drugs are about the same strength. Patients tend to know roughly how sensitive they are to medications and can give guidelines as to where to start. Initial sedation is a significant problem and the more sensitive a person is to medications the greater the sedative effect. Unless sedation is extreme it is not practical to try to change the initial dosage for the first three days, after which the sedative side effects should have dissipated.

Although the manufacturers of the three major BDZs discuss going up to a maximal dosage of 10 mg in 24 hours, I have rarely found any benefit in going above 4 mg in 24 hours. Usually I find optimal therapeutic benefit at a dose of 2 mg in 24 hours or less. If I do not obtain a satisfactory result at 4 mg, I generally stop BDZs entirely and reassess my diagnosis rather than to increase the dosage further. A total dose of less than 2 mg in 24 hours is most desirable. Above 2 mg if the patient stops taking BDZs abruptly, then there is a dose related risk of seizure. Below 2 mg abrupt stopping of the drug has not been reported to cause seizures. Seizures aside, the 2 mg in 24 hours dosage seems to be an optimal upper limit for most people.

When prescribing a BDZ there should be a great deal of dosage adjustment because there is a wide range of effective dosages. One of the most common mistakes doctors make is to prescribe a dose that is too low. Patients are able to accurately tell whether or not a specific dose is too strong or too weak. When patients report that the dosage is too low, doctors sometimes misinterpret this as drug tolerance. Tolerance for panic disorder patients tends to occur over a period of months. Doctors fear that if the dosage will rapidly escalate out of control. When treating a cluster of panic attacks tolerance is exceptionally rare. This can happen if the BDZ is inappropriately prescribed for anxiety related to an individual's personality, for insomnia unrelated to anxiety or for people with primary drug addiction problems.

Patients tend to have spontaneous panic attacks at roughly the same time of day. The most common times are on awakening in the morning, late afternoon and after going to sleep. The dosing should be specific, with exact times of day to take each tablet. A higher dose should be taken prior to the time of day or night most likely to be associated with panic attacks. At other times, a lower dose may be better in order to avoid sedation.

Medication doses should be taken at specific set times. A typical schedule might be about a half hour after awakening, another in the mid to late afternoon and the last dose about a half hour before the desired bedtime. Sometimes the effects are not the same at different times of day. For example, some people may find the midday dose too sedating although the morning and evening doses do not seem sedating. In this case I would cut the midday dose in half.

Since nocturnal panic attacks are so common, I often prescribe a stronger dosage before going to sleep. This is not to be mistaken for using the BDZ as a sleeping aid. Without doubt patients will sleep better when their anxiety is treated, however, if the BDZ is taken exclusively as a sleeping pill tolerance will build rapidly. In other patients the morning dosage needs to be the largest one. It is highly variable. Conceptually, the idea is to take Xanax on a fixed, regular schedule and then to modify the time and size of the dosage to minimize side effects.

Underdosing is more of a problem than overdosing. Certainly you want to keep to the lowest effective dose, but all too often physicians prescribe suboptimal dosages because of fear of addiction. The dosage range is variable and the physician needs to be flexible in schedule and dosage.

The Switch to 'As needed'

The nervous system can get overexcited and stay in that state even though the precipitating stress is gone. The whole point of BDZ treatment is to eliminate that state of overexcitement, to "reboot" the nervous system so that it can return to the normal baseline and then the BDZs can be withdrawn. Still the tendency toward overexcitement under stress is going to persist. When I write about stopping BDZs, what I mean is stopping the regular dosage—not necessarily stopping entirely. Once the nervous system is calmed, it is not necessary to continue regular dosages of BDZs. Instead, the BDZs can be used as needed—not as needed after a panic attack occurs, but as needed when the sensation of an impending panic attack is building. For some the building sensation of tension is progressive insomnia, for others it is irritability and for still others it can be periodic palpitations or heartburn. The symptoms are going to be different from person to person, but my patients seem to easily recognize that sense of mounting stress. When this sensation of being stressed occurs it is appropriate to take a single dose of BDZ.

When using BDZ as needed the dosage will be quite low. A dosage of as low as .125 mg is sometimes effective. A dose of O.25 mg to 0.50 mg is adequate when taken as a single dose although up to 1.0 mg is needed in some people. Generally the as needed dosage is going to be sedating so it should be taken towards bedtime or at a time when possible drowsiness is not a problem. Occasionally it is necessary to take this dosage daily for two consecutive days. A low dose of BDZ can be safely taken about twice a week without a dependency developing. It is more common for a patient to only take an as needed dose of BDZ every few weeks or every few months.

Sometimes the nervous system does get overexcited to the point where clusters of attacks are happening and it is necessary to restart a regular daily dosage for a while. It does not appear that taking BDZs on a daily basis will prevent the recurrence of panic attack clusters when under stress. People who take a regular daily dose of BDZ and have clusters of attacks still need to transiently increase BDZ dosage. Going on and off BDZs gets easier for people over time. Having gone through withdrawal once, future withdrawal experiences get easier. The placebo expectations in BDZ withdrawal are enormous so if a person has had successful withdrawal with tolerable discomfort, then subsequent experiences with stopping BDZs are progressively less distressing.

Chapter XX: Tapering and Stopping BDZs

Knowing how to stop BDZs is as important as knowing how to prescribe them. The information in this section applies in general to all of the BDZs but will be most specifically directed towards alprazolam.

Almost all standard protocols suggest a gradual but rigid tapering schedule. These sort of tapering schedules were primarily developed for drug addicts who are self administering BDZ for non-medical purposes. Greater flexibility can be provided to patients who have been taking BDZs as prescribed on a regular schedule.

The common protocol for tapering BDZs is that after a dosage change, one would stay at this dose and wait for the discomfort to recede before lowering the dose further. What I found when I tried to follow this was that the initial reductions seemed to work pretty well. However, as people moved towards the lower doses they became increasingly uncomfortable. At doses of 0.5 mg or less per 24 hours, patients remain very uncomfortable and as long as they may wait, comfortable adaptation to these low dosages does not seem to occur.

Since adaptation occurs at the higher dosages, it seemed logical to assume that adaptation will also occur at the lower dosages. This, however, is not the case. At the lower dosages one need not wait to become comfortable before stopping completely. It is counterintuitive, but it is only after stopping completely that the discomfort finally goes away.

As far as the speed of the tapering, I have found it to be so highly variable that I have no one schedule. I usually suggest cutting the dose in half over the first two weeks and then dropping by either .25 mg or .125 mg a week after that (see sample schedule). Throughout the tapering process, patients can take small extra BDZ dosages when withdrawal symptoms are too uncomfortable. BDZs seem to have different effects at different times when taken as treatment and this seems to be the case when withdrawing.

Almost all drug-tapering schedules have been designed for addicts. With an addict, any extra drug taken during the weaning process results in a return of the full addiction. For example, if an alcoholic gets even a single shot glass of liquor during withdrawal it is almost a foregone conclusion that they will return to prior full tilt drinking habits. I think that this is also true for BDZ addicts but not for patients dependent on BDZs taken as prescribed. As opposed to dependency on prescribed BDZs, addiction includes all of the behaviors involved in obtaining the drug, the emotions involved in using the drug and the behaviors that surround drug use. This greatly complicates stopping the drug and mandates a chemical dependency model of treatment. For patients who have been taking BDZs on a regular schedule as prescribed, a flexible tapering schedule that allows for extra dosages is usually the best approach and does not result in drug craving.

In patients who are taking BDZs at fixed doses at regular times of day, taking an occasional extra .25mg or .125 mg to reduce withdrawal symptoms (usually for irritability, insomnia, muscle aches or shakiness) does not interfere with the weaning process. So if in the tapering schedule a person needs an extra dose to relieve excessive discomfort, this is not a problem. After taking the extra dose one resumes the schedule. If this is a persistent difficulty the schedule should be revised. As part of the tapering process it is important not only to reduce the quantity of medication at the fixed dosage, but also

139

to stretch out the time between dosages. For example, if the dosage is .25 mg three times a day, one might wait as long as possible before taking the midday dosage. Eventually the midday dosage will be moved back so close to the evening dose that it can be dropped out entirely. For a person on alprazolam 0.5 mg three times a day a typical suggested tapering would be:

Starting schedule: 0.50 mg 0.50 mg 0.50 mg

Week one: 0.50 mg 0.25mg 0.50 mg

Week two: 0.25 mg 0.25 mg 0.50 mg

Week three: stretch mid dose until it drops off at night dose

Week four: 0.25 mg 0.50mg

Week five: 0.25mg 0.25 mg

Week six: 0.125 mg 0.25 mg (one week—some stop here)

Week seven: 0.125 mg 0.125 mg (one week—more stop here)

Week eight: none

Another typical tapering schedule might be:

Week one: 0.50 mg twice daily

Week two: 0.25 mg in AM, 0.5 mg in PM

Week three: 0.25 mg twice daily

Week four: 0.25 mg daily

Week five: none

Patients are seen weekly during the tapering process and encouraged to go at a pace that seems comfortable. Some people have very mild withdrawal symptoms and proceed more rapidly than the proposed schedule and others go more slowly. A permissive, loosely structured withdrawal seems to be the most successful.

The most common symptoms of withdrawal are insomnia, tension headache, irritability, appetite loss, diarrhea, sound sensitivity, smell sensitivity, taste sensitivity and a sense of tremor. If a patient shows visible tremor I assume that the withdrawal is too fast and the dose of BDZ is increased. The withdrawal symptoms generally last for about 5 to 10 days at their most intense and then gradually go away over the next week or two. Some mild symptoms can persist for several months after the last dosage.

On the Internet certain web sites describe a "protracted withdrawal" syndrome that lasts indefinitely. I have not seen this and it is not in the literature. The Internet information on BDZ withdrawal is extreme and seems most appropriate for BDZ-addicted people rather than people taking BDZs for discrete periods of time at fixed dosages.

Chapter XXI: Treating Reflux

My clinical and research experiences show that almost all patients who are having panic attacks bad enough that they require medical treatment also have reflux. Reflux should be treated at the same time as the treatment for panic attacks.

Reflux is often confused with anxiety. Patients seem to get used to the constant discomfort and experience it as a sense of worry. Nervous stomach is felt as a mental sensation of anxiety over time. I have seen patients who initially did not feel that they were having any stomach or esophageal discomfort. It was only after treatment that these people realized how much of what they thought was anxiety was really reflux related symptoms.

Reflux in panic disorder is often a result of bile flowing backwards from the small intestine into the stomach. Bile dissolves the mucous barrier that lines the stomach, making it sensitive to the effects of the hydrochloric acid that is produced by the stomach. Also bile itself is a powerful irritant to the stomach, causing further release of acid and more irritation. Because bile is alkaline, the stomach produces even more acid to neutralize the alkalinity. So bile both irritates the stomach and stimulates acid release. When the stomach fills with acid then the acid, and sometimes both acid and bile, may go up the esophagus causing a variety of problems.

The primary neurotransmitter/hormone responsible for the release of bile is cholecystokinin (CCK). The BDZs act to chemically oppose the action of cholecystokinin. So BDZs themselves may reduce release of bile and help relieve bile-related gastritis and reflux.

The symptoms of reflux are varied. Classically it is experienced as burning pain in the upper abdomen: heartburn. In younger people reflux can feel like hunger. Morning headache, dry cough, wheezing, and asthma-like symptoms are also common symptoms of reflux.

Years ago I regularly referred my patients for endoscopy (looking into the stomach with a fiber optic scope) for panic-related heartburn. It became clear that inflammation of the stomach and esophagus were extremely common. Keeping track of 81 consecutive patients referred for endoscopy I found that all of them had endoscopic evidence of gastritis and reflux. I really consider gastritis and esophagitis to be a part of the stress involving clusters of attacks

that require treatment.

Posted to the PDI bulletin board May 2001 by 2L8
     "I can't stand it anymore. I go from one to the other. Either I
have heartburn or I have a sinus infection or I have panic attacks.
I'm never OK. It goes on an on and on!"

This person, a 38-year-old construction worker, was incredibly

annoyed. He spent his time going from the gastroenterologist to the

ENT doctor to the psychiatrist. He was extremely frustrated with his

inability to be free of this triad of problems. It is documented in the

literature that reflux can manifest as either heartburn or sinusitis, but

usually not both at the same time. It is particularly confusing that

reflux is not consistent and it does not occur in parallel with panic

attacks. Treatment for reflux helps panic attacks, heartburn and sinus

infections.

In some patients who don't want to take any sort of mind-

altering medication I have treated the reflux alone and found that the

patient may experience significant improvement in their anxiety. I

consider treatment of gastritis and esophagitis to be an essential part

of the treatment of panic disorder. In treating reflux, I have had quite a few patients who no longer had problems with other manifestations of reflux such as sinusitis or chronic cough.

If a patient has panic disorder of sufficient intensity to warrant treatment with a BDZ, then I usually consider a trial of treatment for reflux to be worthwhile. Even if it doesn't help it is safe and unlikely to cause harm. On the other hand, many patients will have become accustomed to living with their reflux-based heartburn, sinusitis or cough and attribute the discomfort to their mental anxiety. For these patients treatment of reflux is an important part of treating panic disorder.

Sucralfate

Sucralfate is a relatively inert product that forms a protective seal over areas of damaged stomach and esophageal mucosa. It is the basic drug that I use for panic-related reflux. I have viewed endoscopies performed after the ingestion of sucralfate and observed that it very specifically coats areas that have been damaged, somewhat similar to a bandage. It promotes healing of the underlying gastric tissue. It is not absorbed into the system, but just lines and coats the stomach and esophagus where it has been damaged. It also binds to bile and renders it less caustic. Sucralfate is manufactured in one-gram pills. It also comes in a liquid suspension. These need to be taken on an empty stomach or else they end up coating the food you have eaten instead of your stomach. A half-hour before meals or an hour after meals is usually sufficient for the stomach to be emptied. Because most of the reflux damage occurs during sleep, it is best to take two pills before sleep, one pill on awakening and another pill in the late afternoon. Initially these should be taken on a regular, daily basis and then later they can be taken on a reduced schedule. Relief can be expected as early as the first day of taking sucralfate, although it is more common for it to take a few days to a week before symptoms are significantly improved. After about two weeks to a month the gastric and esophageal lining is usually healed and sucralfate can be taken either as needed for distress or as one tablet before sleep.

Because it is not absorbed into the system, sucralfate has very few side effects. Once again I want to emphasize that any symptom that occurs after taking a pill that was not present prior to taking the pill should be considered a side effect. With this in mind, my experience is that some people have experienced constipation and I have read of allergic reactions but have not actually seen this in practice. Sucralfate can inhibit the absorption of some other drugs and this needs to be considered in patients who are taking other medications. These include: cimetidine, digoxin, fluoroquinolone antibiotics, ketoconazole, l-thyroxine, phenytoin, quinidine, ranitidine, tetracycline, theophylline and some of the drugs prescribed for immunodeficiency disease. A small number of patients have complained of nausea or stomach pain after taking sucralfate. This is uncommon and when it happens I usually obtain a gastroenterology consultation to assess for possible problems beyond just reflux.

The combination of BDZ and sucralfate has been the mainstay of the treatment that I provide to my patients with clusters of panic attacks.

Proton Pump Inhibitors (PPIs)

This category of drug shuts down the ability of the stomach to make acid. Some proton pump inhibitors include Prilosec, Prevacid, Nexium, Protonix, and Acifex among others. Some of my patients have reported that they have an exacerbation of their panic attacks after taking Acifex. In some people who have more severe gastric discomfort I add these to the sucralfate. Usually I will try sucralfate alone first. The proton pump inhibitors are a decidedly second tier drug for my patients when compared to sucralfate. They are effective at reducing excess acidity but do nothing to help with bile reflux. Also, I have found that when these drugs are used on a chronic basis they may cause rebound acidity when they are stopped. For this reason some people find PPIs difficult to stop. Many physicians are prescribing PPIs for years at a time. The safety of PPIs over years has not been established. Certainly the stomach was designed to make acid and stopping acid production entirely is going to interfere with digestion and nutrient absorption. I prefer to use these drugs on a short-term basis only. For patients with more advanced gastritis and esophagitis the combination of sucralfate and a PPI has been helpful.

H2 Receptor Blockers

This category of drug blocks the histamine receptors that are involved in acid production. Examples of these drugs are Tagamet, Zantac, Axid, and Pepsid. These drugs may provide a very temporary relief, however tolerance to the effects of these drugs develops rapidly and they are usually too weak to make much of a difference in panic disorder related reflux.

Motility Stimulators

Motility stimulators, in general, are to be avoided. One of the most common agents of this sort is Reglan (metoclopramide). This is an agent that facilitates the speed with which food passes through the stomach. It also may act by increasing the strength of the gastro-esophageal sphincter. Unfortunately it is a dopamine-blocking agent, and can have side effects similar to the anti-psychotic medications. Side effects tend to be most pronounced the longer it is taken and the higher the dosage ingested. These side effects include a sense of intense restlessness. This is known as akathisia, which is difficult to distinguish from anxiety. Movement disorders such as Parkinson's disease, dystonia and tardive dyskinesia can develop. Parkinson's is characterized by rigidity, resting tremor and difficulty initiating movement. Dystonia involves muscle stiffness, pain and involuntary movements. Tardive dyskinesia involves involuntary movements of the tongue fingers and sometimes the breathing muscles that may have an onset years after stopping Reglan. Reglan is sometimes prescribed for years at a time and over time the dosage is often gradually increased. Most physicians are not aware of the neurological side effects of this drug.

Another commonly prescribed motility stimulator is Bentyl (dicyclomine). This drug is an anticholinergic agent. Side effects of this agent may mimic the symptoms of panic attacks, such as racing heart and anxiety.

Chapter XXII: Selective Serotonin Reuptake Inhibitors (SSRIs) and Other Drugs

This is the category of drug that is most likely to be prescribed to a patient diagnosed as having panic disorder. The drug companies have heavily promoted SSRIs. They are promoted as non-addicting and having almost no side effects, however, this is not the case. In their marketing they simultaneously warn about the addictive properties of Xanax. It is common for physicians to insist that patients take SSRIs and equally as common for physicians to insist that patients not take Xanax.

Posted to the PDI bulletin board on March 2001 by Angry Mom!
My daughter has Panic Disorder and our family doctor just retired. In a quest for a new doctor to treat her we have been met with the worst practice of medicine I have ever seen. My daughter tried the SSRIs and could not take them so our old doctor tried Xanax and she got along so well on Xanax that he said that he would leave her on this medication long term. He was really impressed with her progress on Xanax! NOW, we go to try and find a new doctor and he tells us NO Xanax, he says he will NOT prescribe Xanax because he says Xanax is too addicting. I tell him that in the 3 years my daughter has been on Xanax she has not developed a tolerance, he stutters a bit and then says he does not know enough about panic disorder to treat her. WELL, just out of curiosity I ask him, will you prescribe an SSRI for her Panic Disorder? Now get this, he says YES! I don't even bother to answer him, just escort my daughter out the door.

153

Originally developed as antidepressants, SSRIs are now generally considered a first line of treatment for all anxiety problems. Drugs in this category include Zoloft, Paxil, Prozac, Luvox, Celexa, Lexapro and Effexor (this is a slightly different category of drug but it has similar effects). I am cautious when working with these agents because 1) they may aggravate panic attacks 2) they have too many side effects 3) they can be addictive long term. In some people this category of drug has been very helpful in stopping attacks and in relieving worry. In other people the SSRIs have precipitated some of the worst panic attacks that they have ever experienced. The long-term issues of dependency and tolerance are poorly understood. Clinicians who often treat these problems as new or 'breakthrough' mental illness and prescribe even more drugs to the detriment of the patients.

Case Study: Julie
Julie, a 33 year old attorney and mother of two had been having panic attacks sporadically over the last few weeks. Her family physician was sympathetic and gave her Paxil. He told her that the medication gave some people stomach upset, but otherwise it has no side effects. She left the office with a bag of samples.

The next day, after work, she took the first tablet. Within the hour she was pacing, agitated and noticed tremor of her left hand. The night after her second dose she had a severe panic attack and went to the emergency room because she felt that she might be having a heart attack. Assured that her heart was okay, she was given a prescription for a dozen alprazolam (Xanax) tablets and told to use them very sparingly because they were dangerous and addicting. She used one that night with good symptomatic relief and put the remainder away.

When she returned to her doctor, he assured her that without the Paxil she would have been worse and that she should keep taking it because it usually "takes a few weeks to kick in." The dose of Paxil was increased. After another week of feeling like she was going to jump out of her skin, having more panic attacks, and worse tremor in her left hand, she returned to her family physician. He changed the medication to Celexa, informing her that it had fewer side effects. Julie found that the agitation, tremor and sexual dysfunction were less but still present and she started to develop the sensation of electric shocks running down her arms and the back of her neck. Once again she called her doctor, but this time he didn't answer the phone. Instead she spoke to the office nurse practitioner who told her to stop Celexa and prescribed both Zoloft and Serzone. After two more days, all of her side effects were worse, and she was also lethargic and was no longer able to go to work. Meeting with her doctor again, he prescribed Zyprexa. This time Julie looked it up in the Physician's Desk Reference, and seeing that it was an antipsychotic with a multiplicity of side effects, she never filled the prescription.

Julie's experience is all too common. Often when a patient has side effects from one SSRI, the doctor often prescribes another SSRI. Physicians tend to minimize SSRI side effects hoping that they will go away. Some side effects will go away over time, but many will not.

Although they affect serotonin, these medications do not actually increase the amount of serotonin in the brain. Their mechanism of action is actually unknown. You may hear the phrase "chemical imbalance" used in regards to this category of drug. There is really no such thing as a scientifically defined chemical imbalance. It is a phrase used by psychiatrists to try to make sense of current prescribing practices. These drugs are often referred to as "serotonin boosters" however these drugs actually deplete total brain serotonin. These are probably the most successfully and vigorously marketed drugs in the history of medicine. Over and over the physicians are told by pharmaceutical company-based educational activities that these drugs, unlike the benzodiazepines, are not addicting and that they have *no* side effects. It is emerging that they are probably equally or more addicting than the benzodiazepines. A particularly dangerous side effect of this category of drug is that they can cause a person to develop suicidal thinking. When most physicians are confronted with SSRI tolerance or dependency they increase the dosage of the drug or layer on other, more toxic drugs. This is an important consideration because the SSRIs are almost always prescribed long term.

No studies exist to document what happens when these agents are taken for years at a time. My experience is that tolerance often develops and that over a period of months or sometimes years, the dosage is gradually increased. Some people stay on a dose of a SSRI just to treat withdrawal symptoms. When the dose relieves withdrawal symptoms then the patient may confuse this with treatment of depression or anxiety. Eventually SSRIs become ineffective. The standard psychiatric strategy at this time is to switch to another SSRI in hopes that it will be effective. Occasionally this will work, but often the patient spends months or years being moved from one SSRI or antidepressant to another with little or no benefit. Eventually the patient is put on several medications that are fundamentally treating the long-term side effects of the SSRI. Often this includes the BDZ that was avoided in the first place.

Because SSRIs will aggravate panic attacks, a BDZ is often prescribed along with the SSRI. The theory is that the BDZ will provide relief until the SSRI "kicks in." My preference is to just use the BDZ to provide relief and then to stop it once the nervous system has calmed down and to skip the SSRI entirely. All too often the patient ends up taking both the BDZs and the SSRI together long term.

After years of taking SSRIs at high dosages they can be extremely difficult to stop. Claims are made that these drugs are not addicting but the most recent clinical information indicates that they are addicting. My experience is that the withdrawal symptoms can be incapacitating and can persist for months or-rarely -indefinitely. Some people find symptoms so severe that they are unable to stop taking them. Additionally, the withdrawal symptoms include prominent anxiety and depression that is often mistaken for relapse or "emergence" of underlying pathology.

Another concern is that I have seen SSRI induced mania in people with panic disorder, particularly if bipolar disorder runs in the family.

Posted to the PDI bulletin board October 1999 by Layla:
    I was recently hospitalized for bipolar II disorder, although my current psychiatrist thinks that my life is a mess because I have

situational depression. I can attest to the fact that antidepressants can cause manic depression in people who are being treated for panic disorder, as I have the signs of bipolar disorder while on and while coming off SSRI antidepressants. Recent articles I've read on the subject support this. Caution must be used when treating patients who suffer from panic disorder and from bipolar disorder with antidepressants. I'm sure that's the reason for my 70-pound weight loss and the sleepless nights I spent in my manic phase. I'm now in the depression phase, but I plan on using therapy to help me through the depression and help me get my life back on track. No more SSRIs for me! The current losses I've suffered in my personal life because of my manic behavior and now my depression are too great for me to risk being on those meds again.

Clinicians are generally not informed about the side effects and withdrawal effects of SSRIs and usually interpret side effects as relapse or development of new illness.

SSRI side effects

Within the first few doses you may experience a preoccupation with suicidal or violent thoughts. This occurs in people who were never suicidal prior to taking the SSRI. The preoccupation is intense and unremitting. Suicide seems natural and important and thoughts dwell on the many ways in which it can be accomplished, (I could jump into traffic, I could jump out the window, I could drown myself, I could shoot myself.) This is a fairly common side effect—in as many as 10% of people who take them.

.   The SSRI drugs are addicting. Over time there is a tendency to increase the dosage to maintain the effect. The higher the dosage and the longer you take the drug, the more intense the withdrawal syndrome will be. Some people find withdrawal intolerable and are unable to stop or reduce the medication.   So-called withdrawal symptoms may sometimes occur at a stable dosage even without reducing the dosage. The SSRIs are often used long term in patients, commonly for years at a time. The withdrawal symptoms may result in anxiety and depression worse than symptoms for which it was initially prescribed. Typical withdrawal symptoms are:

Vertigo, ringing of the ears and dizziness

Electric shock-like sensations, most commonly in the head, neck and shoulders (zaps)

Nausea and vomiting

Flu-like symptoms

Nightmares and insomnia

Irritability

Severe depressive syndrome with characteristic crying spells in response to sad or happy emotions

New onset of anxiety or panic attacks

The SSRIs often make anxiety and panic attacks worse when first taken. Be prepared to have more frequent and more intense panic attacks when you start the SSRI drug. The addiction potential of SSRIs appears equal to the benzodiazepines. Instead of prescribing a benzodiazepine to counter the increased panic attacks precipitated by the SSRIs I prefer just using one of the benzodiazepines alone. Weight gain is common. Initially the SSRIs drug may cause weight loss due to nausea and other GI complaints. Rapid weight gain is common later on. A gain of as much as 20 to 30 pounds a year or more is not uncommon. This seems to be due to metabolic slowing rather than appetite increase, so the weight is usually put on despite maintaining the usual diet. Sexual dysfunction is also common. Interest in sex is often reduced or disappears entirely. The most common difficulty is inability to reach orgasm. Some people will find that this goes away with time. However in other people the problem is progressive and they may not return to the baseline even when the drug is discontinued. This is more serious than most doctors realize. Sex can be an anxiety-relieving experience and is an important factor in marital intimacy.

SSRIs may cause akathisia. This is a powerful restlessness where one feels the urge to move yet actually moving does not satisfy this urge. Sometimes people describe this as a sensation that their bodies are moving on the inside. This is extremely uncomfortable and has been associated with suicide and aggression. This symptom can persist after stopping SSRIs.

SSRIs can cause dystonia, a painful stiffness of the muscles that worsens with activity. This can persist after SSRIs are stopped and there is no known treatment. SSRI induced dystonia usually improves over a period of years.

SSRI can cause Parkinson's syndrome. This can persist after the drugs are stopped although it usually goes away within a few weeks after stopping the SSRI. As opposed to idiopathic Parkinson's, which is progressive, SSRI induced Parkinson's syndrome tends to improve over time. Tremor is a common side effect and usually goes away when the drugs are stopped.

Read the manufacturers information on side effects: hundreds of side effects are reported. Common side effects include headache, nausea, drowsiness, anxiety, depression, agitation, insomnia, bizarre dreams, appetite loss, diarrhea, dry mouth, sweating, dizziness, seizures, memory loss, and a rash among others. Physicians often will ignore side effects or deny them. The best way to know if a symptom is a side effect is to stop the drug and see if the symptom goes away. The drug can then be restarted to see if the presumed side effect returns. This test, retest strategy is the only way to properly assess for side effects.

Additional Drug Considerations

I think that certain drug categories require special mention. Older antidepressants of the tricyclic category and the monoamine oxidase inhibitors clearly have a place in the treatment of panic disorder. These drugs are not as useful in acutely stopping attacks and may initially aggravate panic disorder, but they have been enormously helpful to many people over the long term. They have a lot of side effects that tend to keep people from being able to tolerate them. If you can tolerate side effects and can wait a few weeks for therapeutic effect this category of drugs can be useful.

Depression is a common problem in panic disorder patients. Most of the patients that I see have some degree of depression due to the experience of panic disorder. Usually when the panic attacks and GERD are treated mood is significantly improved. Insight oriented and supportive psychotherapy is my first choice for treatment of depression.

Doctors may use any of the antidepressants agents to treat panic disorder and of these, Wellbutrin seems to require special caution. Wellbutrin has seizure as a serious side effect and I have observed it to cause panic attacks in people without prior panic disorder. I suggest avoiding Wellbutrin as a primary treatment for panic disorder. Remeron is another antidepressant commonly prescribed. It is a sedating drug and I have heard from some patients that they feel more relaxed taking this. It does nothing for acute attacks. Any antidepressant is potentially going to be prescribed for panic disorder. Use of antidepressants can be of value, although these are mostly a "try it and see what happens" sort of medical treatment.

Panic disorder is something like a seizure so the anticonvulsants can potentially be of help. None of these drugs have been proven to treat panic disorder. Neurontin, a very mild anticonvulsant, is fairly sedating and some patients find that this is useful in controlling anxiety, but not panic attacks. Dilantin has helped some people. New anticonvulsants that enhance GABA activity such as topirimate and pregabalin are being promoted as antipanic agents but so far it is unclear whether these will be useful for panic disorder. A variety of anticonvulsants that affect the GABA system have been developed and are currently being studied as potential treatments for panic disorder.

Opiates such as Demerol, Morphine, and Vicodin can be very helpful if used cautiously. The major side effect of these drugs is rapid development of tolerance and dependency. In extreme cases I have prescribed opiates and they have been of significant benefit to carefully selected patients. Still, addiction is common and these agents need to be used with caution and careful medical observation.

Amphetamines deserve mention here also. One would think that amphetamine would cause hyperarousal and aggravate panic attacks. This is certainly the case for some people, but I have also treated patients who found that amphetamine made them calmer and seemed to prevent attacks.

Antipsychotics, particularly the newer ones such as Zyprexa, Seroquel and Risperdal are being advocated as treatments for panic disorder. These drugs will stop panic attacks although they are still less useful for acute attacks than a BDZ. This category of drug was used for anxiety decades ago and abandoned, because of the high degree of side effects, in favor of the BDZs. These new antipsychotics have less of the usual antipsychotic side effects that the older drugs caused, such as Parkinson's, tremor, akathisia, tardive dyskinesia and dystonia. These same side effects are still a problem. This category of drug can also be very difficult to stop if taken over a long period of time. In certain, very severe, situations where the patient is not responding to BDZs and there is a question of psychosis these can be useful agents. Zyprexa, interestingly enough, has a BDZ-based molecular structure. Zyprexa is probably the drug that causes the most weight gain of any of the antipsychotics. It also may cause diabetes. All of the older antipsychotics such as Haldol,

Stelazine and Thorazine will also control panic attacks although it is unlikely that these would be prescribed. The potential side effects of the antipsychotic drugs—old and new - are enormous. Some side effects such as involuntary movements may not become apparent for months or years after taking these drugs and they can be severe, disfiguring and disabling.

For me it boils down to using BDZs to control acute attacks. This treatment works rapidly with few side effects for most of the patients that I see. If it does not work, I tend to reevaluate my diagnosis and treatment. If discomfort is extreme and BDZs do not work I may suggest any of the sedating drugs such as Neurontin or Remeron and in the most extreme cases I may try Zyprexa. By the time I start working with these other agents I am generally changing my diagnosis. Many episodic mental disturbances can appear similar to panic disorder. Schizophrenia and manic psychosis may present initially as panic attacks. Many personality disorders also commonly have episodes of intense anxiety.

There are new psychiatric drugs coming out every month. I have only named a few of the best-known drugs here. My general opinion is that panic disorder is not a condition that lends itself to experimentation. As far as a drug to stop the out of the blue, spontaneous panic attacks, I find that Xanax or Klonopin or other BDZs are the most effective drugs with the least side effects. If they do not work, the trial and error sort of psychopharmacology has limited usefulness in panic disorder. All too often the trial and error approach leads to worsening of panic disorder. If drugs are ineffective, psychotherapy alone with lifestyle modification is the next best treatment.

Chapter XXIII: Diet, Exercise, and Supplements

Food and exercise are two areas in which a person can make specific choices to maximize their health. Anything that promotes health is going to have some degree of benefit for panic disorder.

Besides trying to rid the diet of gluten, there is no other specific diet treatment for panic disorder. Good nutrition and good eating habits are going to help keep you comfortable. People need to experience for themselves how they are affected by various foods. Patients often describe a sense that they feel weak or lightheaded if they do not eat at regular intervals. Some patients eat small frequent meals and avoid eating a lot of carbohydrates for that reason. These feelings do not necessarily correlate with measurable blood sugar abnormalities.

Panic disorder patients are generally very sensitive to the environment, and food is definitely a part of the environment. Patients often speak of symptoms occurring after eating. In my practice I have learned that patients sense how they feel after each meal. Clearly after a very large meal most people have a certain sense of fullness discomfort, but in a person with a tendency towards panic disorder large meals can precipitate a panic attack. Large meals aside, individual foods can precipitate either panic attacks or a general sense of discomfort that may approximate a panic attack.

People with panic disorder tend to have allergies. Panic attacks can be precipitated by food allergy or intolerance. Skin testing and other tests for allergy are only useful insofar as they confirm or fail to confirm an clinical allergic response to a food. A positive skin test does not diagnose an allergy in the absence of clinical allergy. In this regard allergy testing may do a disservice to a patient who may have many false positive responses. Similarly a person can be adversely affected by a food without a positive allergy test.

Gluten restriction

My advice for any patient with panic disorder is that they should do a trial of wheat restriction and restriction of the major protein in wheat, gluten. This is so important that I consider it one of the possible treatments for panic disorder. By restricting gluten from the diet some patients can be completely rid of panic attacks. Gluten is not only allergenic, but it is a psychotropic molecule that has stimulating properties. Gluten allergy is common, but gluten intolerance without allergy is probably more common. It only takes 3 to 6 days of gluten restriction to find out if gluten is a problem. Gluten is so ubiquitous that it is beyond the scope of this book to outline a gluten free diet. Many websites can advise on how to restrict gluten. I usually refer my patients to *celiac.com* for this information.

In its most extreme, gluten allergy can lay to waste the entire small intestine. This is referred to as celiac disease. In the United States most celiac disease is not diagnosed until the small intestine is damaged and malabsorption of foods results. In other countries celiac disease is diagnosed much earlier based on clinical findings that are very similar to panic disorder.

Exercise

Like food, exercise is not a treatment, but is beneficial. The effects of exercise, rapid heart, sweating, and rapid respiration, can be similar to the symptoms of a panic attack. These sorts of exercise-induced changes can be mistaken for the symptoms of a panic attack.

Using exercise to bring on these physiological changes can serve as a therapeutic tool to assist in learning how to tolerate these symptoms without attaching danger to them. Very intense exercise can precipitate panic attacks. If this occurs, it is best to reduce activity and then more gradually increase it. Stopping exercise completely for fear of a panic attack is probably counterproductive.

Exercise has beneficial effects on mood. Vigorous exercise induces a more immediate sense of well being. Regular exercise promotes an enduring sense of well being. Knowing that the cardiovascular system is in good shape makes it less worrisome for people when they feel anxiety related chest pain or palpitations.

As with diet, there is no single exercise plan for panic disorder. I do encourage patients to include exercise in their overall treatment plan. Exercise should be vigorous enough to raise a mild sweat. I advise patients to exercise at least a half hour a day for three or four days a week. For people who are sedentary, the easiest way to build exercise into a treatment program is to start walking. It has a low incidence of injuries and can be fit easily into a busy schedule. Walking also counteracts agoraphobia. My patients tell me that it can be difficult to leave the house to go for a walk, but once they have it can help make their make agoraphobia less of a problem for the remainder of the day.

Nutritional supplements

To date I have not found that nutritional supplements are effective anti-panic agents, however some of my patients find various different supplements helpful. I generally encourage patients to use nutritional supplements if they are so inclined because they have so few adverse reactions. Nutritional supplements are molecules already found in the body. This is in contrast to herbs, which are plant molecules that are not naturally in the body. Patients seem to have different responses to a variety of herbs and supplements so the herbs and supplements described are by no means the only ones that might be helpful.

S-adenosyl methionine (SAM-e) is an excellent agent for depression and also reduces interattack anxiety. It is an amino acid derivative found in every cell in the body. It has been extensively studied and it has been proven to be a highly effective antidepressant. The exact mechanism of action of SAM-e is not known although it is thought to support brain function by its methylation effects. Methylation is the process of transferring a basic structural component (the methyl group) from one molecule to another. Neurotransmitters are the products of methylation reactions. The donation of methyl groups also affects energy production and DNA metabolism as well as other biological functions.

Whatever the mechanism, SAM-e it has been extensively studied for its antidepressant effects and found to be equally as effective as prescription antidepressant drugs. As an antidepressant the dosage ranges from 400 to 800 mg daily taken in a single dose. As a general supplement the dosage is 200 mg daily. It is usually taken in the morning because some people find it stimulating. Taking vitamin B-complex with SAM-e facilitates its effectiveness. SAM-e has very few side effects. Usually it is either helpful or it is ineffective. When side effects do occur, they are short lived. Side effects include headache, lightheadedness and insomnia. It should not be taken if a patient has a history of manic episodes as it has been reported to precipitate mania in people with a history of bipolar disorder.

Taurine is an amino acid that has the ability to reduce electrical activity in cell membranes similar to anticonvulsants and BDZs. Taurine is concentrated in the brain where it acts as a neurotransmitter with calming effects on the central nervous system. Taurine is also concentrated in heart tissues where it helps the heart muscle to contract properly, and may be helpful in reducing palpitations. It should be taken on an empty stomach. The usual dosage is 1000 mg once or twice a day taken with a piece of bread or a few crackers.

Carnitine and Coenzyme Q-10. are involved in the production of energy within the cells. Carnitine carries fatty acids into the cell. Coenzyme Q10 (CoQ10) is involved in the process of converting the fatty acids into energy. These supplements do not act like stimulants or make people feel "speedy" although they can boost stamina and help with anxious fatigue. The heart has the highest concentration of CoQ10 of any organ in the body. By increasing the heart's pumping strength and efficiency it is thought that this can be helpful for palpitations and mitral valve prolapse. Taken together, CoQ10 and carnitine work synergistically to help the heart produce energy more

175

efficiently. The dosage of CoQ10 is 30 to 90 mg daily in a singe dose. Carnitine should be taken at a dose of at least 500 mg two times a day. Carnitine should not be taken at the same time as Taurine because they compete for the same mechanism to transport them into the cells.

Kava Kava, the Piper methysticum plant, is reputed to have anxiolytic, anticonvulsant, sedative and muscle relaxant effects. The chemical action of Kava Kava is disputed, but it is thought to be similar to the BDZs. Kava Kava is not effective for stopping panic attacks but is an effective agent to reduce anxiety. The side effects of kava may include scaling of the skin, rashes, involuntary movements and liver toxicity. Serious drug interactions can occur when Kava Kava is combined with BDZs, sleeping pills or antidepressants. Kava Kava is best used intermittently to assist in relaxation, but it should not be taken with any drugs. The dosage will vary depending on the preparation and your sensitivity. It is best to stay under 400 mg of kavalactones, the active ingredient of Kava Kava. The dose of kavalactone per pill is usually on the label.

Valarian root is commonly used as a sleeping agent although it is reported to help with anxiety as well. It does not work as an antipanic agent. Its mechanism of action is not really known however it seems to have anti-convulsant properties. Like Kava Kava it should not be taken with any sedating medications.

Chapter XXIV: Some comments on psychotherapy

Whole books have been written about the various therapy strategies useful for panic disorder. I consider psychotherapy to be a very important aspect of treatment.

As a condition that straddles the mind/body interface, panic disorder can be treated through psychotherapy as well as with drugs. When the goal is to stop clusters of spontaneous attacks, BDZs are the most useful approach. Stimulus-related attacks can benefit from a BDZ but they can also be treated with psychotherapy alone. Stopping attacks is only one treatment goal, and other aspects of panic disorder need to be addressed through education and psychotherapy.

Prescribing psychiatrists who also do psychotherapy are increasingly hard to find. Newer psychiatric training programs may even omit psychotherapy. There is no substitute for interaction with the patient to evaluate how they are responding to treatment. In this sense, I feel that even the drug evaluations should be structured as a psychotherapy appointment with at least 45 minutes of doctor to patient contact time. The placebo value of the drug is powerful and is highly influenced by the relationship between the prescribing doctor and patient.

Therapy aside, it takes me an hour to learn how a prescribed drug is affecting the patient. A fifteen-minute examination with a few questions such as "how are you doing" is generally insufficient to learn how a patient is really reacting to the BDZs or any drug. One way to learn about the patient is to ask direct questions, another is to spend some time interacting with the patient and make observations.

The development of phobias and situational panic attacks are common. In many patients, once the attacks are stopped, therapy is rendered unnecessary. In others, therapy is needed to educate the patient about their condition and to deal with anticipatory symptoms and phobias.

The single most important component of psychotherapy is reassurance. Patients seek out physician contact and therapist contact for reassurance that they are not medically ill and that they are not going crazy. Frequently reassurance is all that is needed for psychotherapy.

Drug prescription alone is not the best possible treatment. Beyond reassurance that insanity and imminent death are not problems, patients want tools to deal with their anxiety.

Abraham Low, M.D., founder of the self-help organization Recovery, Inc., offers some useful tools. The patient should be aware that the symptoms of anxiety are uncomfortable but not dangerous and that they do have the capacity to tolerate the discomfort. Understanding and believing this is a major aspect of the struggle to cope with anticipation-related panic anxiety. He also advises patients to do the things that they fear and hate to do. This recommendation is the key to dealing with agoraphobia and avoidance behaviors. Dr. Low advises patients to endorse themselves for the things that they can do and try to do and to realize that as strange as the experience of anxiety may be, it is all a part of the average experience of being human.

These words of advice are axiomatic principles in all forms of psychotherapy for panic disorder. Here are some common styles of psychotherapy used for panic disorder:

Cognitive Behavior Therapy

Cognitive Behavior Therapy (CBT) has as its premise that the person has made a mistake concerning the perception of their symptoms. The concept is that the person with panic disorder is misinterpreting normal sensations or attaching inappropriate danger to their sensations or thoughts. In this therapy, panic attacks are sometimes induced and then the patient is taught to learn to alter their interpretation of physical sensations or to basically to tolerate their discomfort. Panic attacks have a wide range of severity and it is cruel to induce the most powerful seizure-like attacks. Also, in some people, inducing attacks only seems to facilitate future attacks. Furthermore, some patients are overtly resentful when told that their perceptions and feelings are wrong. I do not favor CBT as a means of stopping attacks.

Many modified forms of CBT do not involve direct induction of panic attacks but do emphasize techniques and strategies to learn to deal with the discomfort of panic attacks, the negative thinking, the phobias and anticipation.

CBT can be a useful and practical form of therapy. An example of a CBT strategy would be cognitive correction for "what if" thinking. First, a person has to learn to identify their tendencies and episodes of "what if" thinking. Once identified, there are four basic steps to keep this pattern of thinking under control. 1) What is the worst that can happen in this situation (what am I most afraid of)? 2) What can I do to prevent this from happening? 3) Have I done all that I can do? 4) If I have done all that I can and should do, then I can lay this concern aside. This is just one of a variety of strategies that can be used to alter thinking patterns that are working against the patient's best interest.

Anticipation can be helped by modification of belief systems. This happens naturally to some extent when people have stopped the major attacks with a BDZ and have been educated to realize that their anticipation is bringing on symptoms. People have a very natural understanding of how their own anticipation is bringing on certain symptoms and education about this phenomenon alone is therapeutic. Cognitive behavioral therapy can help people to better learn not to attach danger to their sensations and how not to bring on anticipation related symptoms. Learning to tolerate discomfort is critical to functioning with panic disorder. Uncomfortable sensations are going to occur, and it is important to be able to tolerate discomfort at times. A large variety of self help books that emphasize CBT techniques are available.

Exposure Therapies

In this type of therapy the patient deliberately exposes themselves to situations that are known to produce anxiety. Continued exposure is meant to facilitate desensitization to the feared situation. This is a useful tool for overcoming avoidance and phobias. It is often used in conjunction with CBT. For example, some people have panic attacks when they go to shopping malls. If that is the case, going to the shopping mall and gradually spending increasing amounts of time there can reduce or eliminate the discomfort of being in a mall. Exposure to the shopping mall is combined with the use of CBT techniques to help deal with the discomfort. Some therapists will actually go with the patient to the mall to facilitate exposure. Similarly, a person who gets symptoms when they are driving the freeways can drive increasing distances on the freeway until driving is

comfortable again.

Find a Support Network

Nothing is more helpful than a good support group. Even one

good friend who has panic disorder can serve as a small support

network. Group therapy for panic disorder is generally not viable; the

groups do not tend to last long as groups of people are often

uncomfortable and patients tend to drop out after a few sessions.

Recovery Inc. is a nationwide group that promotes "mental health

through will training." It is for all sorts of mental problems but often

the groups are highly focused on anxiety and panic disorder. They are

a nationwide organization so individual meetings can vary widely.

Recovery Inc. can be strongly opposed to medications or biological

concepts of panic disorder and this can be a problem.

In my Panic Disorders Institute website I have a discussion

forum that has served as a support group. Ongoing for the last 7 years

and with a significant number of my people participating, I know first

hand that an Internet support group can be enormously helpful. It is a virtual community and it is also a place where you can be introduced to people who you might contact separately via e-mail or telephone.

Contact outside of the Internet with other people who have panic disorder is often initiated by Internet contact. It is useful to have a real friend with panic disorder that you can interact with and share your thoughts, experiences and feelings. To learn of the experience of panic disorder in other people is one way to understand your own experience. Sharing your fears, phobias and odd sensations with another person who is having similar symptoms lessens the sensation that you are totally alone in your problems and allows for sharing of various coping and adaptive strategies. It also seems to foster a sense of humor about the human condition in general and panic disorder in particular.

Analytic Therapy

This sort of therapy looks at how your past influences your current thinking on an unconscious basis. It looks at your style of how you handle life situations. This is the old-fashioned insight oriented therapy. Because panic disorder is a stress responsive condition, understanding what pushes your buttons is clearly going to help you to deal with your life stressors and thereby ameliorate the effects of stress on your nervous system. These sorts of therapies are necessarily open-ended. You do not use this sort of a therapy to eliminate any one symptom. The only goal is understanding. Understanding your emotional make-up should help you to be more resilient in the face of anxiety and more flexible in your ability to adapt to new situations. Everyone has fears, conflicts, fantasies and unconscious motivations. Exploring this aspect of the unconscious is one of the best ways to reduce stress on the nervous system.

Formal psychoanalysis is done three to five times weekly. Modified analytic styles of therapy usually involve sessions every two to four weeks. In the modified analytic styles, often referred to as dynamic therapy, unconscious beliefs, personality style and enduring patterns of behavior developed early in life are explored. Many patients will engage in this sort of therapy for a period of months and then stop therapy when it feels natural. When symptoms are worse or if there is a period of stress or crisis therapy is resumed. Panic disorder aside, this sort of a therapy would probably be invaluable for anyone. This is the standard therapeutic style that most psychiatrists of my generation were trained in.

Take a Look at Yourself

Often the patients who present with a cluster of panic attacks are having a personal crisis. Sitting down with a therapist, a neutral helping party, can assist a person in examining their lives and the current factors that are affecting them. Relationship issues are the most common sort of problems that aggravate panic disorder patients. Bad marriages or abusive family situations can be an enormous stress. The next most common problems relates to work issues. Overwork and underemployment are both enormous stressors. Basic counseling can help you examine your life to see if you have serious stressors that you are avoiding.

The Kitchen Sink

People with panic disorder often suffer so severely that they are eager to do whatever they can to feel better. They are ripe for all of the therapists who claim to be able to heal and cure panic disorder. If you are not careful they will throw the kitchen sink at you in the name of treatment. Just as every new medication is given to patients with panic disorder every new therapy is tried on patients with panic disorder. Panic disorder is a serious and complicated condition. Thus far, therapists who claim that they have found *the* cure have been wrong, and some of them have been outright quacks. No other condition in the world is so vulnerable to exploitation. Claims of new and vaguely biologically-based therapies for panic disorder are common and unlikely to be of benefit. CBT, dynamic psychotherapy, exposure therapies and counseling therapies are probably the best choices.

Mantra Meditations

Meditation is the focus of attention on a thought, an object or an activity. Mantra meditation is the focus of attention on a word or sound that is repeated mentally or verbally. This sort of meditation has been shown to relax the autonomic nervous system. It is also good training to break away from obsessive anxious thinking patterns.

The technique is simple. A single word or simple phrase is mentally affirmed over and over. Many people use the word relax or peace. You can choose any word or phrase that appeals to you, and you can change this any time. This word is the mantra. Usually the mind will drift away from the phrase and return to thoughts related to anxiety. When this occurs and you realize that you are no longer saying your mantra, you then return to repeating the mantra.

By exerting your will to let go of anxious thoughts and to focus your thoughts on your mantra you are consciously saying no to the repetitive themes of worry. This particular technique is very useful at night when anxious thoughts tend to surface. It is useful for getting to sleep. It is not always easy but as time goes on it becomes more natural to let go of anxious thoughts and return to the mantra.

This sort of mantra meditation is worth practicing. Initially you may only be able to do it for five or ten minutes, but with practice you should be able to last for over a half hour. Later this technique can be used informally whenever you realize that you are having unpleasant anxious thoughts.

Chapter XXV: Is this an Inherited Condition?

The answer to this is yes and no. My theory is that panic disorder is an interaction between stress and vulnerability. Some people will have low vulnerability to panic disorder but with sufficient stress they will develop it. Other people have a high vulnerability and develop panic disorder in response to seemingly minimal stress. The predisposition of a person to react to stress with panic attacks seems to be inherited. In a subset of people that I refer to as having "generational panic disorder"(GPD) the person has a predisposition to panic attacks with minimal stress. GPD seems to show an autosomal dominant inheritance pattern. That means that a parent with this problem would have an even chance of passing the problem on to a child. It also means that each person who has it has a parent who has it. Statistically, half of the parents' siblings will have it and half of the patient's siblings will have it and half of the patients children will have it. In GPD the condition does not tend to skip generations.

Panic disorder can run in families. While it may be obvious in some families, in other families it can be a well kept secret. Denial about familial illnesses is enormous.

Posted to the PDI bulletin board May 1999 by Day Tripper;
I got it from my dad, who got it from his mother. She was severely disabled by it, stopped leaving the house in her 20s and is now in her 90s. My father got around more, but always suffered from anxiety and panic.
I didn't "tell" my parents about my PAD; they told me. I was seven or eight years old, standing in the hallway on a sunny afternoon shaking and crying and swearing that I must be dying and begging them to let me run somewhere while simultaneously saying that maybe I was going to throw up. By the second or third of these, if not after the first, they told me that I had the family curse, "anxiety neurosis" they called it then. They said I could expect a lifetime of misery, that I might be in and out of mental hospitals, but that I shouldn't feel ashamed, because it was biochemical.

Day Tripper's experience is unusual. Families don't tend to be so honest in discussing these sort of problems with children. Denial is the rule rather than the exception.

I was an investigator in a study on patients with Huntington's disease. This is a frightening and crippling autosomal dominant neurological condition with progressive dementia and flailing movements of the extremities. Like GPD, each child has a 50% of having it. It was fascinating to see that even something this obvious, a progressive and horribly disabling disease, was not openly discussed

in the family and was often denied in the face of obvious symptoms.

The research experience with Huntington's Disease taught me what

an autosomal dominant neurological condition looks like in family

structure. When I observed the family dynamics of patients with

Huntington's Disease I realized that the families of some patients with

panic disorder shared many of the same features.

Posted to the PDI bulletin board on March 2000 by Sybil

My maternal grandmother had PAD/Agoraphobia - so bad she
never left her house during the last 16 years of her life. Her
daughter (my mother) also suffers from panic, phobic avoidance and
depression (but adamantly state's: "I'm FINE!"). Go figure...

Now here is the interesting bit:

Both my brother and I have been diagnosed with PAD. We are
14 months apart in age (my brother is older) - and the onset of
symptoms occurred at almost *identical* times in our lives, e.g. when
we reached 30. I had not even seen him in 4 years because I am in
Australia and he is in LA. I started talking to him about my
"problem" - that's when he *spilled* the beans to me about his
situation. Needless to say we concluded there *must* be a genetic
component.

Sybil's experience is typical of the denial that often runs in

families. Sometimes during the initial interview, patients tell me that

the condition does not run in their families. Later, if they ask their

family members, they learn that a parent had this problem for a while when they were in their twenties (and that they still carry around an old Valium that they have had for 20 years). Brothers and sisters may be seeking medical specialty evaluation for various aspects of the somatic manifestations of panic disorder and never realize that they have similar conditions.

Some patients feel that they do not want to have children to avoid the possibility of giving panic disorder to the child. It is more of a consideration when the condition is severe and easily observed in multiple family members. How the tendency towards panic attacks is expressed is highly variable and development of panic attacks is also dependent on life experiences. Another consideration about having children is that people who have a tendency towards panic disorder tend to be sensitive and creative people who may be able to use these traits to great advantage as writers, artists or as good human beings. So a child with the tendency towards GPD can have special gifts.

Chapter XXVI: A consideration of the children

Children with GPD tend to be misdiagnosed as ADHD. In younger children anxiety commonly manifests as restlessness and poor concentration in school. Such children tend to have unique personalities, which can be misinterpreted. Unfortunately children are diagnosed with ADHD when their actions are in conflict with the expectations or demands of parents and teachers. This is a mistake. Instead of examining why the child is restless or disobedient in the classroom or home, the problem is attributed to the child's faulty brain. The fit between the child's temperament and classroom or family circumstances may not taken into consideration. One of the most common reasons for a child to become restless in school is the stress of divorce or other family problems.

It is all too common for these children to be put on Ritalin or other amphetamine products. This does not address the problem and just drugs the child into a more compliant and submissive state. Stimulant medications suppress spontaneous behaviors and increase compulsive and focused behaviors. Schools and overworked parents often welcome this. Once prescribed, they are almost always used long term. Stimulants can cause panic attacks, insomnia, chest pain, stomachache and other symptoms of anxiety. Depression, apathy, tics, tremor or even psychosis can result as well.

Stimulants also seem to be a 'gateway' drug, and children placed on stimulants are often subsequently placed on other psychiatric drugs such as antidepressants or mood stabilizers to deal with side effects of stimulants or other undesirable behaviors. It becomes a vicious cycle of trying to drug the child and drug the side effects of the last drug.

If there is a strong family history of GPD there are steps to take to optimalize their health. You cannot know whether a child is going to develop panic disorder in advance so these steps are good ones for healthy children as well.

• Start children early in high quality childcare for very brief periods of time. The point is to gradually get the child used to the experience of separation. Many of the good childcare programs transition the child into separation by having the parents stay in the facility while the child is encouraged to explore and play.

• Face the critical issues on education. Any child will do better in teacher and child-friendly classrooms with more inspiring curriculum and smaller classes. If a teacher gives you the blunt choice of putting your child on a drug or leaving the school, then you should strongly consider a new school.

• Accept that children develop at different rates in different skills. Do not become overly alarmed if your child's skills lag behind others.

• Take a critical look at your own home. Make sure that your child getting the love and attention that he needs.

• Make sure that your child's diet is not the problem. See if restricting wheat gluten, refined sugars and milk makes a difference. Look for other possible food allergies.

• Enjoy your child for who he is. Children with GPD tend to be creative, intelligent and loving. They have gifts, not always obvious, that need to be fostered.

• Above all, avoid drugging your children. As far as treating panic disorder I do not use drugs for children unless there is no other choice. There is no real literature that suggests that the current trend of psychiatrists to drug children is scientifically valid. This should be a choice of last resort. Focus instead on identifying the genuine needs of your child in the school, home and community.

Chapter XXVII: Pregnancy

Anecdotal reports and case studies have described a reduction in the severity and frequency of panic symptoms during pregnancy. This has also been my experience with patients. Some patients have told me that pregnancy was the most comfortable time of their lives. The impact of pregnancy on panic cannot be definitely predicted, although I think it is safe to say that many pregnant women do seem to have a remission during pregnancy. Hormonal changes may ameliorate anxiety. Progesterone, in particular, has metabolites that possess barbiturate-like activity and may be anxiolytic.

In making decisions regarding the treatment of women with panic disorder who are pregnant or planning to conceive, the clinician must discuss not only the risks associated with prenatal exposure to various psychotropic agents, but also the consequences of untreated panic disorder during pregnancy. Untreated anxiety symptoms may cause significant morbidity in the mother and may also have an effect on fetal outcome.

Panic attacks during pregnancy are not necessarily benign. Panic attacks are associated with increased stress hormones. Although the impact of these hormonal changes on fetal well-being has not been well studied, it is common sense to avoid being over stressed while pregnant.

There are also data to suggest that untreated anxiety during pregnancy is associated with poor fetal outcome, including preterm labor, low birth weight and other obstetrical complications. While most of my patients do well with pregnancy, for those who have continued problems with anxiety it is probably better to continue medications than to stop them.

Patients with panic disorder who are maintained on antipanic medications and who wish to discontinue pharmacotherapy prior to attempts to conceive should be advised to taper medications slowly just as they would if they were not trying to get pregnant. Some women have very comfortably done a faster taper shortly after becoming pregnant. Women who attempt to taper and stop drugs in anticipation of getting pregnant will have a more difficult time than women who taper and stop drugs after they get pregnant.

Some women may elect to continue BDZs during pregnancy. No medication taken during pregnancy is completely without risk, however it seems that BDZs used for panic disorder are usually not associated with adverse effects on the baby. The risks associated with untreated panic disorder need to be weighed against the risks of fetal exposure to a particular psychotropic agent.

The consequences of prenatal exposure to benzodiazepines have been debated for 20 years. Three prospective studies failed to show increased risk of organ malformation following first-trimester exposure to BDZs. Still, there are studies that support and some that fail to support an increased risk of cleft lip and palate. The issue of risk remains unresolved but fetal abnormalities due to BDZ use are uncommon.

Neonatal toxicity as well as symptoms characteristic of withdrawal have been described following benzodiazepine exposure at the time of delivery. This has been in case reports, but no systematically derived data has been obtained. I have not heard of this happening in my patients who are taking the standard dosages of BDZs.

The postpartum period appears to be a period of increased vulnerability to panic and depressive symptoms and many women with panic disorder may elect to use antipanic medication after delivery. All the psychotropic medications are secreted into the breast milk, but concentrations vary widely. Effects on the newborn are variable, but have a low frequency of severe complications. Clearly breastfeeding has many benefits for both mother and infant, and the use of psychotropic medications usually should not preclude breastfeeding. If questions arise, the infant's plasma may be assayed for the presence of drug.

In short, if you are pregnant, you may well be able to stop medication for the duration of the pregnancy. If you need to continue medication, it appears that untreated panic disorder is equally or more damaging than using a medication.

So if you get pregnant…Don't worry about it.

Chapter XXVIII: Family Dynamics

Marriage

Panic disorder can present some unique challenges in marriage. The afflicted partner will tend to be seen as "negative" and "controlling." The negative part comes from the anticipation of possible disasters or adverse life experiences. So if a couple is planning a vacation, the spouse with panic disorder may well verbalize many fears about the vacation. The afflicted spouse may just say that they are not interested in a vacation to avoid their concerns. They may be preoccupied with questions such as "will we get to the plane on time, will the plane be OK, will I need to get off the plane and be unable to do so..." It is typical that people with panic disorder find themselves more concerned about the financial aspects of a new car than the pleasure of the purchase. Preoccupation with the possible adverse consequences of an event seems to be part of the disposition of a person with panic disorder.

To the spouse with no panic disorder the afflicted spouse seems like a bad sport. While the spouses with panic disorder may see themselves as concerned about possible dangers, to the non-afflicted spouse this appears to be negative thinking. Because people with panic disorder have so many special needs, such as frequent breaks when driving, avoiding certain restaurants, inability to go out for seemingly no reason, food requirements, allergies, and sound and light sensitivity to name a few examples, it may seems as if the person with panic disorder is excessively controlling. Of course, it can be a real source of security to the spouse of a person with panic disorder to realize that every possible problem has already been considered for them in advance.

Several difficulties can arise within the context of a marriage. Because a person with panic disorder has so many concerns, the spouse may discount anything that the patient says, considering it to be part of the panic disorder and not a valid personal concern. Marriage breaks down quickly when the spouse with panic disorder has an issue to discuss and the other spouse replies, "Did you forget to take your medicine?" The patient may be in a loveless or abusive marriage and strongly desire a divorce but can be unable to tolerate the potential stress of separation. Inability to travel or enjoy vacations can be a source of irritation to a panic disorder patient's spouse. Clinging and neediness can become a burden as well.

In general I find that people can be sympathetic to an acute illness, but they tend to grow less sympathetic over time to those with chronic illnesses. When a patient with panic disorder invokes their illness as a reason that the spouse should compromise, gradually sympathy tends to be replaced with irritation. This tends to foster a viewpoint that all of the patient's wishes and needs are considered to be part of the illness. At times it is necessary to invoke the needs of the illness, but in general it is best to deal with comfort on the level of usual human needs.

That is, instead of saying that a certain restaurant is not acceptable because it makes panic disorder worse, merely suggesting that a different restaurant would be more desirable is a better approach. Instead of saying that one feels that driving will aggravate anxiety, rephrasing it as driving seems like "too much just right now" is more socially acceptable. After all, people have differences of opinion and preference. But when a patient invokes their illness too often as a reason for their choices, this becomes an issue of control and not preference.

Over the years I have also observed that the spouse with panic disorder, who is easily irritated and prone to dissatisfaction in general will find their partner to be inadequate and will resent them to a disproportionate degree. It is frustrating to the person with panic disorder that their spouse seems to be unable to comprehend their problems. More marriages are ended by the afflicted partner than by the unafflicted partner. The afflicted partner is sensitive and easily irritated. This innate tendency to be irritated is difficult for the person with panic disorder to distinguish from more overt marital conflict. Marriage takes a lot of work and involves acceptance and compromise from both spouses. Marital conflicts in patients with panic disorder often need to be dealt with in individual therapy as well as marital therapy to sort out the temperament of the patient from the actual problems with the marriage.

Raising children.

As a rule, the parent with panic disorder tends to reject the child with panic disorder. The child with panic disorder may not be manifesting overt symptoms, but may be fussy. It may be that parents are rejecting the part of themselves that they wish to deny. Causation aside, anxious children tend to irritate anxious parents. This is particularly true of parents who have not dealt with their own panic disorder. Parents who have come to grips with their own illness are much likelier to be understanding of an anxious child. In parents who have not dealt with their anxiety I often hear of serious fights and heated arguments between afflicted child and afflicted parent. Parents who have not dealt with their own anxiety are more prone to insist that their child is mentally ill and needs aggressive treatment.

On the other hand, even parents who have a good understanding of their own illness may project their anxieties onto their children. A well-meaning parent may interpret the normal anxiety of childhood as the excessive anxiety of panic disorder. When this happens, the child may identify with the parent and have a learned state of avoidance behaviors. Fortunately the child who is not afflicted with panic disorder will soon find that the pleasures of a more diverse life experience outweigh any inadvertently assumed anxiety.

A problem for the child who is not afflicted with panic disorder is that the healthier child does not get enough attention. Children and adults with panic disorder have very specific and very immediate needs. Often the child without panic disorder is less demanding but at the same time feels as if they are less loved or less important because they receive less attention. They can develop feelings that the family members with panic disorder unfairly control them. This is true of any family structure where one child is ill or handicapped, but in panic disorder the handicap is less obvious. If an agoraphobic parent is unable to attend graduations, weddings or other major events in the child's life then the child may grow up feeling unloved or unworthy of love.

It is difficult to predict which child is going to end up with panic disorder. Childhood is a time filled with anxiety so if a child appears anxious that does not mean that panic disorder is on the horizon. It is not a good idea to try to shelter a child with anxious temperament from all life stresses, as each child needs an optimal level of challenge and frustration.

Chapter XXIX: Too Much of a Good thing

We all need some sort of early warning system. A sixth sense that kicks in to protect us before conscious awareness of danger would be of tremendous survival value. To anticipate danger is good. But to anticipate it too much danger is counterproductive and annoying to the people who do not have panic disorder. There is no objective measure of how much a person should anticipate possible danger. Is the freeway dangerous? Yes. Are crowds unpredictable? Yes. Is air flight intuitively difficult to comprehend? Yes. The question is, to what extent should you alter your behavior and to what extent need you be preoccupied with these dangers.

As a society we are in denial about the complex and enormous dangers all around us. The person with anxiety may be correct about what they fear. But as a society we have to move forward and act as if potential dangers are not harmful. A person with anxiety may anticipate any sort of change with dread and as such they are less able to function in our society.

Someone once said that nothing would ever be accomplished if it were not for optimism. Philosophers and theologians have described the world as being what we project on it. What we expect is what we get. For this reason, it is ill advised to be too cautious, too risk aversive. The world is so unpredictable that we all need to focus on the positive as much as possible. Still, it is almost reflexive for many anxious people to confront novelty, adversity or uncertainty with a negative, defensive reaction. Our innate warning systems are required for survival, but if exaggerated they can ruin the quality of life.

The particular fears of panic disorder commonly relate to the experience of being alone and territorial concerns. It is as if the most primitive, tribal concerns of man are the focus of panic disorder.

Patients feel so much more comfortable if they have companions. It is not just a desire to have help in case of a medical emergency. Patients will use pets or small children as companions and find that they are far more comfortable than they would be without them, despite the fact that these companions would be of little or no help in an emergency. In this regard, some patients find that a cell phone can serve as a companion symbol and make them much more comfortable. In primitive societies being cut off from the tribe must have been a certain prescription for disaster. People with panic disorder have a desire to stay close to their "tribe."

Panic disorder looks as if it has a strong territorial component. For example, if a person has a panic attack while in a restaurant eating ravioli, this person is far more likely to avoid the restaurant where they had the panic attack than they are to avoid the ravioli. Sometimes this person would avoid the dinner company, but this is still much less common than aversion to a location.

These features make the most sense if you think of anxiety in terms of primitive, tribal existence. In a tribal situation people are highly interdependent on each other. No threat could be greater than the threat of isolation from the tribe. Regarding territorial concerns, in primitive circumstances it would be enormously advantageous to have an unconscious, instinctive, sense of which territory is dangerous. When venturing out of the tribal community there would have been territory that was inhabited by a hostile tribes or dangerous predatory animals. Responding to subtle cues of these sorts of dangerous territories would be highly desirable from a survival perspective.

When one considers the stress of primitive man, no threat was greater than starvation. This helps to explain the finding of abnormal bile flow in panic disorder. Bile is used to absorb fat, the most highly caloric of the food components. For those who face possible starvation it would be highly useful to be ready to absorb every last fat calorie. It seems likely that excessive activity of the hormone responsible for fat absorption, CCK, plays a more central role in the causation of panic disorder than serotonin.

Chapter XXX: The Gifts of panic disorder

One of my patients bemoaned, "Am I going to have this disorder the rest of my life?" To this I replied, "no, but you are going to be *you* the rest of your life." The predisposition to be sensitive and highly sensitive to certain stressors is not going to change. Over time people do find a balance between achieving a lifestyle that minimizes the most difficult stressors but allows for engaging in certain activities with discomfort but not illness. Discomfort is not limited to those with panic disorder: Everyone has to tolerate discomfort in their lives in various forms. It is the degree of discomfort that can be comfortably tolerated that may distinguish panic disorder patients from others. Still, all must tolerate the inherent discomfort of living gracefully.

Panic attacks seem to be a common human phenomenon and even those who do not have panic disorder are going to have panic attacks. A nervous system that is more sensitive to stress than average is going to present problems when it is overtaxed, but on the other hand this sensitivity can be a gift. Sensitivity is a desirable attribute in many endeavors, particularly writing and art.

Beyond the medical basics, it is up to each person to establish the optimal care and feeding of the sort of sensitive nervous system that is prone to panic attacks. Panic disorder can result in some dramatic specific symptoms, however it is more than just a disease, it is the temperament of your nervous system.

All humans have, at their core, a desire to live authentically and without apology the life that reflects their highest inner dreams and aspirations. In those with a sensitive or sensitized nervous system, this desire is a primal requirement for acceptable health.

At its most basic and fundamental core, the "disease" of panic is not the problem; the problem is how to fit a sensitive being into a complex world that is not particularly sensitive. Panic disorder does not have to limit a person in their goals, dreams and aspirations. This sensitivity is a gift as well as a source of discomfort. It is an integral part of a person, not something that you cure. Do you have to suffer? No. Can this be a transcendent experience? Yes.

Depending on your situation, sensitivity can be an ugly duckling or a swan. In general, our society favors insensitivity. Much of what we are called upon to do is tedious and boring. But not everything, and not for everyone. Often people with panic disorder are highly creative people. Writers are disproportionately represented in my practice. Finding the right sort of livelihood is important. Many patients tire easily in an externally-paced job situation but find that they have enormous energy for self-paced work. Similarly, my patients find that they become fatigued and have trouble concentrating on boring work, but that if work is creative and meaningful concentration comes easily.

While my primary goal in this book is to inform people of my knowledge of panic disorder to help them obtain maximal health and well being, I want to mention here the intangible aspects of being. I must speak of the spirit otherwise I risk being just another lead weight on the ankle of the person with panic disorder, a scientific version of the many books that promise freedom from fear, the five easy steps to an anxiety-free life; the promise that anyone can conquer anxiety. Certainly it is necessary to be free of disabling physical and emotional symptoms before the more difficult issues of the spirit can be addressed. The spirit can be even more complex than psychological conflict. My patients who have done the best, who are without medications, without symptoms and with minimal anxiety have come to grips with their lives on the deepest possible levels.

With proper treatment and attitude you can be free of panic attacks and other symptoms of panic disorder, but only living in harmony with your world and innermost hopes and fears provides the ultimate sense of calm that people with panic disorder seek. Given this enormous disclaimer, I wish to offer my knowledge and experience to assist patients in achieving the best possible medical care for their panic disorder. I hope that this is also the first step to a deeper personal transformation as well.

About the Author

Stuart Shipko, M.D. is a board certified psychiatrist in private practice in Pasadena, CA. He has treated over 2000 patients with panic disorder. Dr. Shipko has published original research relating panic disorder to reflux related heartburn and sinusitis. Founder of the Panic Disorder Institute website, Dr. Shipko has been a strong advocate for people who suffer from panic disorder.

Printed in the United States
19101LVS00001B/204